Bible Stuff

Spiritual Teaching for Under Fives that's Fun

God Made Our World
God Gives Us Friends

Janet Gaukroger

Contents

God Made Our World

Week 1	God Made Day and Night	4
Week 2	God Made Plants and Trees	9
Week 3	God Made Animals	14
Week 4	God Made People	19
Week 5	God Made Me	24

God Gives Us Friends

Week 1	David and Jonathan	29
Week 2	Four Friends	34
Week 3	Paul and Timothy	39
Week 4	Jesus Visits Friends	44

Introduction

Welcome to *Bible Stuff* – an activity-based curriculum designed to help us communicate spiritual truth to children from birth to age five.

Basic beliefs

There's no doubt that children take in a massive amount of information in the first five years of their lives. Many significant attitudes and habits are formed which will last a lifetime. It is so important that we pass on the Christian faith to our children from the very beginning. We have the opportunity to give them a heritage of spiritual strength. *Bible Stuff* is one attempt to help us make the most of that opportunity by combining a number of factors to produce an effective programme. The programme's four basic beliefs are as follows.

1. Communicating Biblical truth is very important

Bible Stuff is committed to the truth and accuracy of the Bible as God's Word, living and active in today's world. Teaching it to the next generation is a serious responsibility.

2. Teaching in ways that under fives can understand is crucial

We have not effectively taught the Bible if the recipients of our teaching have not learned. We must, therefore, understand where under fives are in their physical, mental, spiritual and emotional development so that we can teach in ways they will relate to.

3. Children learn through play

Recognizing that play is the child's work means choosing activities that are fun, but that are also part of the development process.

4. Children are all different

Providing a variety of activities simultaneously allows a child to express his or her own personality by choosing what to be involved in. (*Bible Stuff* does not recommend everybody doing the same thing at the same time. It recognizes that one child may be happy to play in the home corner for an entire session, and another child may need the stimulation of four or five different things in the same period of time.)

This curriculum has been tried and tested by the under fives teachers at Stopsley Baptist Church in Luton. I owe them a great deal for their loyalty and support over many years.

May God envision, encourage and empower us through his Holy Spirit as we 'tell the next generation the praiseworthy deeds of the Lord' (Psalm 78:4).

How to use this book

Bible Stuff contains two teaching units, one of five weeks and one of four. The story and activities for each week are completely self-contained, though spending four or five weeks on the same theme reinforces the teaching. For each session you will find:

 Preparation

This includes Bible background or a meditation for teachers – we need to feed on God's word ourselves in order to teach effectively.

 Story Time

This section includes a short selection of Bible verses related to the theme of the session. They are paraphrased in language under fives can understand. Use them throughout the session as you talk to and with the babies and children. The more they hear us saying 'The Bible says…', the more they will learn what a special book it is.

Two versions of the Bible story are given each week. One is aimed at babies and toddlers, the other at children aged between three and five. If you have a class that mixes ages you can use either version, depending on the maturity level of your particular group.

Teaching Activities

These are divided into activities for babies, toddlers, 2s – 3s and 3s – 5s. Again, if your class combines ages, choose an activity from each age group. You will find that some of them overlap,

 ## Group Time

There are separate suggestions for 2s – 3s and 3s – 5s. If you are working with babies and toddlers, sitting them all down at once to hear the story is rarely a possibility. Don't worry – you can be telling them parts of the story all through the session. In fact, you can do that with all under fives, so that when they hear the story in group time, it will have a familiar ring.

Take Home!

Each session ends with a photocopiable take-home paper. This is to give to parents or carers and is designed so that they can follow up the teaching at home. It gives the story and Bible verses, then two or three suggestions for home-based activities, at least one of which is suitable for babies. You may need to give some explanation and encouragement to the parents / carers to help them make the most of the take-home sheet.

Planning

Start by reading through the whole unit: some activities require the collection of various items in advance. Also, teachers can share responsibility for bringing any necessary equipment. Some activities are suggested for more than one age group, so if you have more than one class of under fives, co-ordination between groups will help all concerned.

Setting up

If possible, try to have the room ready when children arrive. This creates a more relaxed atmosphere. You do not need a lot of fancy equipment or expensive toys. For under fives, bricks, a simple home corner, puzzles and books should be available at every session. They give a sense of continuity and are also the most-used items for this age group. Don't put out all of your equipment each time you meet. Using the activities suggested for each week adds variety. Look through them to make a basic equipment list.

Group time

Group time comes at the end of each session and is an important part of the teaching / learning process, but it is not the only part. It's to be hoped that teaching will be going on throughout the session in the various activities. Group time should be between five and ten minutes long, depending on the age and maturity level of the children. Its components are conversation, singing, prayer, telling the Bible story and sometimes a 'game' or 'activity'. The order of these components can vary from session to session. Try to choose the moment when the children are most settled to tell the story. Sometimes some of the children may want to pray, sometimes only a teacher will pray. You may find that you need to sing four or five songs to settle children, and another time it will only take one. Try to have several ideas ready for group time, but remain flexible.

Health and safety

Never leave children unsupervised when using sand, water and dough. If necessary, put these items out of reach until you can come back to them. If you are in any doubt about mess, cover the children's clothing with aprons. If you are not sure about safety guidelines, ask someone who is. Check with your local social services office, get information from your local library or make contact with the person responsible for health and safety in your church building.

Resources
The following books offer detailed help and information:
Sharing Jesus with Under Fives, Janet Gaukroger, Crossway Books
Children in Crèches and Toddler Groups, Ann Croft, CPAS

God Made Our World   Week 1

GOD MADE DAY AND NIGHT (GENESIS 1:1-5, 14-19)

Aim To help the children understand that God made day and night; he made the sun, moon and stars.

Preparation

If there is a clear night this week, take ten minutes to go outside after dark and observe the stars. If you have the time, go out into the country to do this, where it is really dark. Observe how many stars there are, and the patterns of the constellations.

During the day, take a few minutes to watch the clouds, or let your imagination play with the shadows made by the sun.

This week, try to notice the sunsets. Consider the wonder of day following night, season after season, year after year. This aspect of creation by itself is something to marvel at.

Find a few quiet moments to read and meditate on Psalm 19: 'The heavens declare the glory of God'. Ask God to reveal his glory to you in a new way this week as you notice day and night, sun, moon and stars.

'*Lord, as I prepare to teach, may I have a new sense of awe and wonder at your creative power. You have made the heavens and they declare your glory. I pray that I, too, may declare your glory today. Amen.*'

Key Bible verses for this unit
The following verses apply to all of the sessions in this unit. Copy and keep them; refer to them as you plan and prepare.

Everything God made was good. (Genesis 1:31)
Every good thing comes from God. (James 1:17)
God gives us things to enjoy. (1 Timothy 6:17)

Story Time

Bible verses
God made the moon and the stars. (Psalm 8:3)
God made the sun to shine in the daytime. (Genesis 1:16)
God made daytime and night-time. (Genesis 1:5)

Birth - 2s
In the beginning, God made the world. God made the sun to be the light. He called the light 'daytime'. God called the dark 'night'. He made the moon and the stars to be in the sky at night.

The day and the night help people to know days, months and years. They also help us to know summer and winter.

God saw the sun, moon and stars that he had made. He saw the daytime and the night-time. He was pleased with what he had made.

Week 1

3s - 5s

In the beginning there was only darkness. Then God made the world. First he made light. He made the sun shine. God called the light 'daytime'.

He called the dark 'night'. God made the moon and the stars to be in the sky at night.

God planned that the day and night would help people to know days, months and years. They also help us to know summer and winter, spring and autumn.

God saw the sun, moon and stars that he had made. He saw the daytime and the night-time. He was pleased with what he had made.

Teaching Activities

Hopefully, as we have meditated on daytime and night-time this week we have been blessed, and thrilled again at the wonder of God's creative power. Let's communicate a simple, but profound truth today: God made the world. With the older children, conversation about what they do in the daytime, about bedtime and about sun, moon, stars and clouds shouldn't be too difficult.

Babies

Make a book of sun, moon and stars Find four pieces of card to make a book. On one page draw a sun, on another draw a crescent moon, on the third draw some stars and on the fourth draw the sun with some clouds. Resist the temptation to draw a face on the sun or clouds – try to draw a realistic picture. Punch holes in the card and put the book together with wool or ribbon.

As you show babies the simple pictures, tell them about God making day and night.

Look at bubbles inside bottles Find one or two small plastic bottles. Put about an inch or two of water inside them, then add a few drops of food colouring and a few drops of washing-up liquid. Screw the lids on tightly. As babies shake the bottles, coloured bubbles will form. For younger babies, you can do the shaking. The general Bible verses for this unit are appropriate to any activity that you are involved in with the babies.

Look at books about day and night If you have a good supply of board books for babies, you may already have one or two that relate to day and night, such as books about bedtime, bathtime, toys or playing. If not, buying a couple would be a good investment. They can be used over and over again.

If the budget doesn't allow for this, you may be able to make a book if you can find suitable pictures in magazines of people involved in daytime and night-time activities. As babies look at pictures in the book, talk to them about things they do during the day, and things they might do at night to get ready for bed (have a bath and a bottle).

Toddlers

Toddlers will enjoy picture books about day and night, as well as bottles filled with bubbly water.

Make a night-time picture with chalk Provide white chalks and black or dark blue paper for toddlers to draw on. They do not have to draw stars or the moon (they can't). They can scribble if that is what they normally do. Chalk dust can be quite messy so you will probably want to provide aprons to cover clothing, and a bowl of water or a damp cloth for cleaning hands. As the children work, you can talk about the dark sky at night and the moon and stars that God made.

Week 1

Look at Bible verses Choose four or five of the Bible verses recommended on page 4 but not all from the same page of Genesis. Make Bible markers out of dark blue or purple paper and put a star at the top of each one. These can be either gummed stars that you can stick on, or home-made white stars that you have cut out and glued on.

Write a verse on each marker and place each one at the appropriate place in the Bible. Even though the children can't read, it is good for them to see the Bible being handled properly. They will gradually come to learn that it says different things in different places. Let the children choose a marker, then read the verse to them. If they will listen, talk about the verse.

2s - 3s

Use Bible markers with the twos and threes today as well, but make the star on each marker a different colour. Cut a large star to match each of those on the markers. Let the children choose a large star, then find the marker that matches. You can make night-time pictures with chalk, too. You may also want to provide gummed stars for the children to stick on their pictures.

Give the baby doll a bath You will need a plastic doll, a towel and something to use as a bath. If you have a baby bath, that's fine, but if not you can use a washing-up bowl. Cover the floor with several sheets of newspaper to absorb the water that is spilt. You can use soap if you want to, but it isn't essential. You might want to provide a small flannel or sponge for the children to wash the doll.

Let as many children as want to have a turn. As you help them wash the doll, talk to them about what they do at night to get ready for bed. Tell them about God making day and night.

Match coloured stars Cut out stars in several different colours and two or three clearly different sizes. Make sure that every star has a match of colour and size.

Let the children match up stars by colour, by size or in pairs of colour and size. As they do this 'puzzle', tell them the Bible verses for today. Save the stars so that they may be used again. This activity will be suggested in Week 3 for threes and fives.

3s - 5s

Make night-time pictures with chalk and stars as an art activity today. You may also want to consider the following ideas.

Pretend bedtime Bring several items associated with bedtime such as a blanket, a pillow, an empty hot-water bottle, a book, a teddy, and some pyjamas or a dressing gown (an older child's size is best – they can get it on over their clothes, but it isn't so big they trip over it).

Put the items in the home corner. Help the children pretend it is bedtime. They may want to act out different things they do to get ready for bed, such as brushing their teeth or having a bath. Let them take turns lying down with the blanket and pillow. As you pretend bedtime, tell them about God making day and night.

Play a daytime / night-time game Make a game about day and night activities. First, cut out two cards which are approximately twenty centimetres square. On one draw a sun, on the other draw a moon and some stars. Make several smaller cards with pictures on them of activities or things to do with day and night, such as cleaning teeth, having a bath, sleeping (a bed), playing, eating, swimming. You can use any number of pictures or activities. You can either draw these or cut them out of magazines. On one small card write 'God made the moon', on another, 'God made the sun' and on a third, 'God made the stars'. Put these in with all the picture cards. Turn the cards face down and let the children take them one at a time and decide which large card to put them on – day or night. Some activities may belong with both.

As the children play the game, tell them today's Bible story.

BIBLE STUFF   *God made our world/God gives us friends*

Week 1

Play with playdough Provide playdough for the children. If you are making it up fresh, make yellow dough. Provide rolling pins and round cutters as well as star-shaped cutters if you have them. The children can make suns and stars if they want to.

As they play, sing to them about day and night and God making the world.

Group Time

2s - 3s

When you are ready to call the children to group time, you could give each one a star, making sure that you have the matching size and colour. Hold up a star, and let the child who has the same one come to the circle, and so on, working your way through all the stars the children have. In conversation, talk about bathing the doll, and what the children do to get ready for bed. Talk about day and night activities.

When you have told the story, sung some songs and prayed (in whatever order seems most natural!), you can let the children choose the stars that match the Bible markers as you wait for parents to come.

3s - 5s

Use all the normal elements of group time today – singing, talking, praying and telling the Bible story. Share the Bible verses with the children. You may want to mark three or four of them in your Bible.

As you wait for parents to arrive you can play the daytime / night-time game.

Playdough - a basic recipe

1 cup of salt
2 cups of flour
2 tablespoons cooking oil or baby oil
2 teaspoons cream of tartar
2 cups of water
a few drops of food colouring

Mix all the ingredients in a saucepan. Cook over a medium heat, stirring continuously. The mixture will form a consistency similar to scrambled eggs and will start to come away from the side of the pan. A lump will form. Remove from heat, allow to cool and knead on a clean surface. Store in an airtight box or polythene bag. Keep in a cool place.

BIBLE STUFF *God made our world/God gives us friends*

GOD MADE OUR WORLD — WEEK 1

Take Home!

GOD MADE DAY AND NIGHT (GENESIS 1:1-5, 14-19)

Aim
To help the children understand that God made day and night; he made the sun, moon and stars.

Bible verses
God made the moon and the stars. (Psalm 8:3)
God made the sun to shine in the daytime. (Genesis 1:16)
God made daytime and night-time. (Genesis 1:5)

The story
In the beginning there was only darkness. Then God made the world. First he made light. He made the sun shine. God called the light 'daytime'.

He called the dark 'night'. God made the moon and the stars to be in the sky at night.

God planned that the day and night would help people to know days, months and years. They also help us to know summer and winter, spring and autumn.

God saw the sun, moon and stars that he had made. He saw the daytime and the night-time. He was pleased with what he had made.

Activity suggestions

Make a book about the sun, moon and stars
Find four pieces of card to make a book. On one draw a sun, on another a crescent moon, on the third some stars and on the fourth the sun and some clouds. Try to draw a realistic picture, rather than drawing faces on the sun or clouds. Punch holes in the sides of the cards and tie the book together with wool or ribbon.

As you show your baby the book, tell him or her about God making day and night. If you have an older under five, he or she might enjoy helping you make the book.

Bath a doll
Let your child bath a doll. If you have a baby bath, you can use that. Otherwise, a washing-up bowl is fine. As you work together to bath the doll, you might talk about various daytime and night-time activities. Tell your child about God making day and night.

Look at the clouds
If the weather is suitable one day this week, go outside with your child and look at the clouds. Sometimes they look like various shapes: encourage your child to use imagination. Say thank you to God for making clouds.

BIBLE STUFF · *God made our world/God gives us friends*

God Made Our World Week 2

GOD MADE PLANTS AND TREES (GENESIS 1:11-13, 29-30)

Aim To help the children understand that God made vegetation – trees and plants; he made some for food, and others for us to look at and enjoy.

Preparation

Pick leaves from three or four different plants or trees. Look at them closely. Notice how they differ in size, shape, colour and texture. Look at the intricacy of the vein pattern on each leaf. What an amazing God we worship!

Read Psalm 95:1-7. Ask God to speak to you from his Word as you sit quietly in his presence.

'*Heavenly Father, sometimes it is hard to be fresh and energetic week after week with the children. Please give me not only physical energy, but spiritual life and vitality as I teach today. Help me to be passing on a living, life-changing faith to the children I teach. For the sake of your Son, Jesus Christ. Amen.*'

Story Time

Bible verses
God made trees and plants. (Genesis 1:11)
God made fruit trees so we could eat the fruit. (Genesis 1:29)
God made trees that were beautiful. (Genesis 2:9)

Birth - 2s
God was making the world. He made trees, plants and flowers. God made big trees with lots of leaves. He made trees with fruit on them.

God made plants. Some plants just had leaves on them. Some plants were vegetables.

God made flowers. He made red, yellow, pink, blue and purple. He made flowers of every colour.

God planned that some trees and plants would be for people and animals to eat.

God looked at all the trees, plants and flowers he made. He saw that they were very good.

3s - 5s
God had made day and night. He had made the sea and the land. God made trees, plants and flowers. He made many different kinds.

God made tall trees with big leaves. He made smaller trees with tiny leaves on them. He made trees with fruit that grows on them.

God made flowers of every different colour. There were pink, red, blue, yellow and purple flowers.

God made plants. Some plants just had leaves. Other plants were vegetables and were good to eat.

Week 2

God planned that some of the trees and plants he had made would be food for the animals. Some of them would be food for people. Some trees, plants, and flowers would be to look at and enjoy.

God looked at all the trees, plants and flowers he made. He saw that they were very good.

 ## Teaching Activities

This unit on creation is fun. There are many good activities we can do. Teaching under fives is serious business – but it can be enjoyable too! Let's ask God to give us a lot of joy and laughter as we teach today.

Babies

Look at different kinds of fruit Bring three or four different kinds of fruit with a variety of colours and textures for babies to look at. Choose fruits that they can handle without making a mess: an orange, a red apple, a kiwi fruit, a grapefruit, a plum – the list is long!

If you have some older babies who you think can manage tasting, you could peel and slice a banana while they watch. If you plan to do this, you might want to put a notice on the door or ask parents as they bring their babies, just to make sure there are no allergies. As babies touch and handle the fruit, tell them about God making trees and plants.

Look at flowers and leaves Bring a variety of flowers and leaves from the garden for babies to look at. It might be a good idea to place them inside a transparent document wallet which can be sealed. In this way babies can look without eating or tearing!

As babies look at flowers and leaves, tell them today's Bible verses and sing to them about the things God has made. Make up songs with a few simple words. If you are not comfortable with making up your own tune, use someone else's! For example: 'God made the pretty flowers, pretty flowers. God has made the pretty flowers. Thank you, God!', sung to the tune of 'Here we go round the mulberry bush'.

Make a book of plants, flowers and trees Look through a gardening catalogue and cut out pictures of flowers, plants and trees. Glue one picture on each side of a card. Make four or five cards. Punch holes in the cards and tie them together with wool or ribbon to make a book. On the front you could write 'God made plants and trees'.

Take a walk if weather permits If the weather is warm and dry you can take babies out for a walk. One adult could take one or two babies at a time, depending on their age, mobility, and the availability of a buggy or double buggy. Alternatively, you could take a blanket outside if there is a grassy area nearby. Let babies play in the warm sun for a little while. While you are outside talk to babies about the sounds they can hear and the things they can see.

As with tasting, it is probably best to notify parents of your plans. Most parents will be delighted, but it's possible that some would rather you didn't take their child outside, and you must respect their wishes.

Toddlers

Toddlers will enjoy looking at different fruits, and they will certainly want to taste them! You might let them taste seedless grapes, banana and peeled apple (only a small bit of each). They will enjoy watching you prepare the fruit for them to taste. You can do this if you have another adult, or few enough children that you can manage a peeler and a knife safely. If you have any doubts, slice some banana and apple before the session for the children to taste.

Week 2

Toddlers will also enjoy going outside if you have adequate supervision. One adult can only manage two toddlers unless you have a safe, fenced-in area. You may want to ask one or two extra people to be ready to assist with this activity if the weather permits. An older teenager or an older adult might enjoy helping for part of one session. As with babies, notify parents about tasting and about going outside.

Make a leaf and flower collage Bring a selection of small leaves and flowers from the garden. (If your own garden supply is limited, you can usually 'borrow' from someone else's garden if you are not too embarrassed to ask!) Provide heavy paper or card to make the pictures. Let children spread glue over the paper with a brush, then choose leaves and flowers to place on the picture surface.

When they have finished, print 'God made trees and plants' somewhere on each picture. (It would seem a time-saving idea to do this before the session, but, inevitably, you find that the children glue over the words!)

Observe leaves and flowers This activity can be used as an alternative to going outside. In addition to the nature items you bring for the collages, collect a variety of leaves and flowers for children to look at. If you have one or two small pot plants that are interesting, you might want to bring those as well.

Place them on a low table or on a large tray on the floor. Let toddlers look at the different leaves and flowers. Talk to them about how God made so many different kinds of trees and plants.

2s - 3s

Observe and taste fruit, and go outside for a walk as described for toddlers. If it is raining, or going outside is not an option because of busy roads or too many children, bring leaves and flowers for children to look at. Even if you do go outside, you may still want to bring items for the children to observe.

Paint with leaves Find some leaves that have long enough stems for children to hold. Longer, narrow leaves will probably be easier to manage than very broad leaves. Provide green paint in a shallow dish and large pieces of paper. You will probably need to help most children wipe the leaf on the edge of the dish as they go to paint, so that the paint doesn't drip everywhere. Let them use the leaves as paintbrushes. As the children paint, tell them today's Bible story. Talk with them about the plants and flowers God has made.

Prepare at home by experimenting with a few different leaf shapes so that you can find which works best. If you haven't enough supervision, try a 'dry' version of this activity by bringing a variety of leaves and letting the children make wax crayon rubbings of them.

3s - 5s

You can use all the activities suggested for the twos and threes today – going for a walk, leaf painting, observing and tasting fruit, and looking at leaves and flowers. If your outdoor space is limited, make the most of it by staggering your groups' outside visits during this session.

Make a garden This is an additional activity for this age group. Bring a shallow box in which to make a garden. The size of box is determined by the number of children who will be involved. If you have a small class, then a box about thirty centimetres square is big enough. If you have more than ten children, you will need a bigger box. Put a layer of soil from your garden in the box, about five centimetres deep.

Cover the working area with newspaper. Bring small twigs (some with leaves on them), flowers with stems, and small stones. Let the children arrange the items in the soil to make a garden. If you are really adventurous you could bring a small shallow bowl and put water in it. Build the soil up around it to make a 'pond' in your garden. Let the children arrange and rearrange the garden as they want to. As they work, tell them about God making so many different kinds of trees, plants and flowers.

BIBLE STUFF   *God made our world/God gives us friends*

Week 2

Group Time

2s - 3s

If it is possible to go for a walk outside, you may want to wait to do so until near the end of the session. Have the children tidy the room for group time as you normally would, only a bit earlier. Take all the children outside together and sit on the grass for group time. Of course, this will only work if there is a fairly quiet grassy area, free from the distraction of traffic and other noise. If in doubt, stay inside for group time.

In addition to singing about the things God has made, you can get the children to do a variety of actions related to trees and leaves – they can wave their arms back and forth like trees swaying in the breeze. They can wiggle their fingers from above their heads down to the floor like leaves falling from trees. They can stoop down curled up in a ball, then open up as they stand, like a flower opening up in the sun.

When the children are ready to sit quietly you can tell them the Bible story. Pray, thanking God for plants that give us food, and for beautiful flowers to look at. If sitting outside, talk to the children about what they can see and hear. If indoors, talk to them about what they saw and heard on their walk.

3s - 5s

Use the same ideas as suggested for twos and threes, including an outside group time if possible.

You may want to place the garden that the children have made in a convenient position so that they can show it to their parents as they leave.

GOD MADE OUR WORLD — WEEK 2

Take Home!

GOD MADE PLANTS AND TREES (GENESIS 1:11-13, 29-30)

Aim
To help the children understand that God made vegetation - trees and plants; he made some for food, and others for us to look at and enjoy.

Bible verses
God made trees and plants. (Genesis 1:11)
God made fruit trees so we could eat the fruit. (Genesis 1:29)
God made trees that were beautiful. (Genesis 2:9)

The story
God had made day and night. He had made the sea and the land. God made trees, plants and flowers. He made many different kinds.

God made tall trees with big leaves. He made smaller trees with tiny leaves on them. He made trees with fruit that grows on them.

God made flowers of every different colour. There were pink, red, blue, yellow and purple flowers.

God made plants. Some plants just had leaves. Other plants were vegetables and were good to eat.

God planned that some of the trees and plants he had made would be food for the animals. Some of them would be food for people. Some trees, plants, and flowers would be to look at and enjoy.

God looked at all the trees, plants and flowers he made. He saw that they were very good.

Activity suggestions

Look at pictures of plants, flowers and trees
Obtain a gardening or seed catalogue and show your baby the pictures of brightly coloured flowers. Tell him or her about God making plants and trees.

An older child who can handle scissors may want to cut out some of the pictures and glue them onto paper.

Make leaf and bark rubbings
Take paper and crayons outside to make bark rubbings from trees. If you do not have any trees in your garden, perhaps you could visit a local park. Let your child collect a few leaves to make rubbings with as well. As you do this, talk to your child about God making plants and trees.

Say it with flowers
Do you know someone who is ill, or perhaps house-bound or lonely? With your child, take a gift to that person of some inexpensive flowers or a plant – from your own garden if possible. Let your child help you choose and wrap the flowers. Perhaps your child may want to make a leaf rubbing picture to accompany the gift.

BIBLE STUFF   *God made our world/God gives us friends*

God Made Our World   Week 3

GOD MADE ANIMALS (GENESIS 1:20-25)

Aim To help the children understand that God made all the animals; that he was pleased with what he had made.

Preparation

Choose one of these activities to help you reflect on the truth that God made all animals and that he was pleased with what he had made.

- Go outside and watch and listen to the birds.
- Visit a farm where it is possible to get close to the animals.
- Watch a television documentary about animals.
- Borrow a book about animals from the library and read it.

In whatever activity you choose, notice the amazing detail of different animals and birds. Think of the intricacy of God's design - not just in appearance, but also in habitat, feeding styles and other special characteristics.

What fun God must have had making all those animals! Which one of us would have thought of such amazing variety? What did Adam think when God brought all the animals to him so he could name them? God is great! He is amazing!

Read Psalm 92:1-4. Meditate on the works of God's hand, not only in creation, but also the works he has done in our lives.

'*Today's session has great potential, Lord, for both chaos and learning! I pray for relative peace when the real animals are in the room, but also for a great sense of fun. Father, in all the excitement of today's activities, I pray that the foundational truth of you creating the animals will come shining through. Amen.*'

Story Time

Bible verses
God made all the birds and animals. (Genesis 2:19)
God made the animals that live in the sea. (Genesis 1:21)
God was pleased with the animals he had made. (Genesis 1:25)

Birth - 2s
God made the animals. He made animals to live in the sea, like fish and whales and dolphins.

God made birds to fly in the sky.

God made animals that walk, run and hop. He made animals that crawl on the ground.

God made very big animals, like elephants and giraffes. He made very small animals, like mice and kittens.

God saw all the animals he had made. He was very pleased.

Week 3

3s - 5s

God had made night and day. He made the sea and the land. He made trees, plants and flowers.

Now God made the animals. He made animals to live in the sea, like fish and whales and dolphins.

God made birds to fly in the sky.

God made animals that walk and run, like lions and deer. He made animals that hop, like rabbits and kangaroos. He made animals that crawl on the ground, like caterpillars and snails. God made very big animals, like elephants and giraffes. He made very small animals, like mice and kittens.

God saw all the animals he had made. He was very pleased.

Teaching Activities

Most children are fascinated by animals. Even babies will enjoy looking at pictures of them, and seeing a small animal up close. Some of the older under-fives may have a fascination with more 'gruesome' animals like spiders, snakes and sharks. We must remind ourselves that God made all the animals, although with some of them we may wonder why! Let's try to steer conversations in positive directions and revel in the amazing creativity of God as he made so many different kinds of animals. If planning a visit from a small animal, you may want to consider notifying parents in advance: some children may have allergies. This activity should be very closely supervised.

Babies

A visit from a small animal No doubt someone in your church or neighbourhood has a small animal such as a rabbit, a kitten or a hamster. It will, of course, need to be a very tame one that is used to being handled. Ask if you may borrow it, or invite its owner to bring it to the class.

Hold the animal so that even the youngest babies can look at it. Older ones may want to touch it. As the babies watch the animal, tell them about God making the animals.

Look at pictures of animals in books If you do not have any animal picture books in your supply, visit the children's section of your library. Choose factual books with photographs, or realistic drawings rather than story books depicting animals involved in human activities or dressed up in clothes. As babies look at the pictures, tell them today's Bible verses.

Play with toy farm animals If you do not have farm animals, you can probably borrow some from a family with young children. Make sure they are big enough so that babies can't swallow them. A horse, a cow, a pig, a sheep and a donkey would make a good selection.

As babies play with the animals, sing to them about the things God has made. For example, 'God has made the cows, God has made the cows; Thank you, God, for making the cows', to the tune of 'The farmer's in his den'; also, try substituting various kinds of animals as you sing 'God has made the animals. Thank you, God, for birds that fly. God has made the animals. Thank you, God, for rabbits that hop', to the tune of the first two lines of 'Twinkle, twinkle, little star'.

Toddlers

Bring books about animals for toddlers today, as well as arranging a visit from a small animal. Someone may have a hamster that has a clear plastic ball in which it exercises. The children will probably enjoy watching it.

Week 3

Play with animals in the sand If you do not have a sand table, use a plastic baby bath or a washing-up bowl to hold the sand. Place the sand container on the floor or on a low table, covering the area beneath with newspaper or a plastic sheet. Put four or five plastic animals in the sand. These could be farm, wild or woodland animals - whatever you have or can borrow. (Avoid dinosaurs – the questions they raise aren't easy to deal with, and some parents may not feel comfortable with their use.)

As children play with the animals in the sand, tell them the Bible story and talk about animals they have seen.

Make an animal collage Cut out magazine pictures of animals, either photographs or realistic drawings. Let the children glue the pictures on a piece of paper. For children this age, it is usually best to help them put glue on the back of the picture, then turn it over and let them stick it down. Even though some toddlers will need a lot of assistance, try to let them do as much as they can for themselves.

When they have finished, print 'God made the animals' or 'God was pleased with the animals he had made' on their picture. Write the Bible reference for whichever verse you use.

2s - 3s

Most children enjoy looking at books about animals, so have some ready for the twos and threes today. Making an animal collage is a further activity you may want to try.

A visit from a small animal is scheduled for all of the groups today. Make careful arrangements with the group leaders and the animal's owner to make the most of each short visit. Between five and ten minutes is usually quite enough for both the children and the animal visitor. Let the older children meet the animal first, with the possibility of a return visit should time allow. Consider inviting two animals and sharing the 'workload' of the visit between them.

Play with animals in water Put a few centimetres of water in whatever container you have to hand. Remember that water splashes out very easily when lots of little hands are in it. Even if you normally use a small bowl for water play, you might want to try to borrow a baby bath to use today so as to give children more room.

Put five or six plastic animals in the water, preferably sea creatures if you can get them. As children play, talk with them about God making all the animals.

3s - 5s

Arrange a visit from an animal, and make collages of animals today. Provide books about animals, too. You may want to visit the library and get some books with photographs. You might be able to find an encyclopaedia of animals.

Play with animals in the brick area Put several different toy animals with the bricks today. Children may want to build pens for them. A teacher may need to stay in the brick area today to encourage wholesome play, rather than animal fights! (Or even arguments between children who are struggling to take turns!)

As children play with the animals, you can talk about animals they like or have seen, and tell them the Bible verses for today.

Play a matching stars game This was suggested for the twos and threes in Week 1. Borrow the stars from the teacher who prepared them at the time. As children match colours and sizes, you can remind them of the stories from Weeks 1 and 2.

BIBLE STUFF *God made our world/God gives us friends*

Week 3

Group Time

2s - 3s

Consider starting or ending group time with a second visit from an animal. Alternatively, you can show the children pictures from the books about animals. You may get more interruptions than usual as you tell the story: the children may want to name other animals in each category. Normally, it is good to try to have children quiet and attentive while you tell the story, but don't worry too much about it today.

After you have told the story, you might want to let the children pretend to be different animals. They can hop or roar as appropriate. Some of the children might want to pray, thanking God for a specific kind of animal. You could even go around the circle, asking each child to name an animal he or she likes, then saying: 'Thank you, God, for making…'

3s - 5s

You can use the ideas suggested for group time with twos and threes today. Children will probably be very responsive, and more than happy to contribute – in fact, you may have a job holding some of them back! You may want to play a game with the stars while you wait for parents to come. Hand them out and let the children see whose star matches theirs. You can repeat this game two or three times.

Beautifully and wonderfully made

You may have children with physical or mental disabilities in your group. They are known intimately and loved completely by God. If you anticipate questions from older children, you may want to ask the disabled child's family in advance about how they would like you to answer those questions.

You will need to be sensitive today to make sure that all the children in your class have a positive understanding that God has made them and that he loves them.

BIBLE STUFF *God made our world/God gives us friends*

GOD MADE OUR WORLD — WEEK 3

Take Home!

GOD MADE ANIMALS (GENESIS 1:20-25)

Aim
To help the children understand that God made all the animals; that he was pleased with what he had made.

Bible verses
God made all the birds and animals. (Genesis 2:19)
God made the animals that live in the sea. (Genesis 1:21)
God was pleased with the animals he had made. (Genesis 1:25)

The story
God had made night and day. He made the sea and the land. He made trees, plants and flowers.

Now God made the animals. He made animals to live in the sea, like fish and whales and dolphins.

God made birds to fly in the sky.

God made animals that walk and run, like lions and deer. He made animals that hop, like rabbits and kangaroos. He made animals that crawl on the ground, like caterpillars and snails. God made very big animals, like elephants and giraffes. He made very small animals, like mice and kittens.

God saw all the animals he had made. He was very pleased.

Activity suggestions
Play with toy animals
If you do not have any toy animals, you may be able to borrow some from another family with young children. Let your baby play with them this week. You may want to set them up with water play one day. You only need a few centimetres of water in a washing up bowl. Put the animals in the water. As your baby enjoys playing with them, tell this week's story.

Get a special animal book
Take your older under five to the library to look at (or even borrow) a book about animals. Find one with photographs rather than drawings. The text might be complicated, but your child will enjoy the pictures. Tell about God making the animals.

Many families enjoy visits to farms and zoos. If you do take your child, make the most of this natural opportunity to use Bible verses or tell about God making the animals.

BIBLE STUFF — *God made our world/God gives us friends*

God Made Our World week 4

GOD MADE PEOPLE (GENESIS 1:26-31; 2:15-25)

Aim: To help the children understand that God made people and that God loves people.

Preparation

Sometime this week, when you're in a crowd, take a few minutes to watch people. Notice how God has made us all so different – not only different faces and bodies, but even different fingerprints! God continued his creative variety when he made people. None of us looks the same, and our personalities all differ as well.

Read Matthew 6:25-34 and think about how much God loves people, the crown of his creation.

'Father, I pray that as I teach about both your creativity in making all people, and your love for all people, I might be filled even more with your compassion. As I watch people this week, please soften my heart. Help me to see them as Jesus saw them, like sheep without a shepherd. Then, Lord, turn my compassion into action in sharing my faith and meeting practical needs. Amen.'

Story Time

Bible verses
God loves people. (John 3:16)
God made a man and a woman. (Genesis 1:27)
God knows all about everybody. (Luke 12:7)

Birth - 2s
God had made the world. It was beautiful. There were trees and plants. There were lots of animals. But there were no people.

So God made a man. His name was Adam. God brought all the animals to Adam so he could decide what to call them.

Then God made a woman. Her name was Eve. Adam and Eve lived together in the beautiful world God had made.

There were fruit trees and vegetable plants for Adam and Eve to eat.

God told them: 'I want you to be happy in the world I have made. You will have children. The animals will have babies. You can live together in the world I have made.'

God looked at everything he had made. He looked at the people he had made. God was very pleased.

3s - 5s
God had made the world. It was beautiful. There were lakes and rivers. There were trees and plants. There were lots of animals. But there were no people.

So God made a man. His name was Adam. God brought all the animals to Adam so he could decide what to call them.

Week 4

But Adam was the only person. God did not want Adam to be alone, so he made a woman. Her name was Eve. Adam and Eve lived together in the beautiful world God had made.

There were fruit trees and vegetable plants for Adam and Eve to eat.

God told them, 'I want you to be happy in the world I have made. You will have children. The animals will have babies. You can all live together in the world I have made.'

God looked at everything he had made. He looked at the people he had made. God was very pleased.

Teaching Activities

Today we want to continue our emphasis on creation as we think about God making people. We have the story of Adam and Eve, but we also want to teach that God made all people, and that he loves all people.

Babies

Look in a mirror Bring a mirror for babies to look in. A smaller, hand-held mirror is all you need for younger babies. For older babies you might want to bring a bigger mirror as well, so that they can see all of themselves in it. It is advisable to use child safety mirrors for this activity.

As babies see their reflection in the mirror, tell them about God making people.

Make a picture cube of people Use an empty tissue box to make a picture cube. Cover it with plain paper. On each side glue a picture of a person. If possible use pictures of people of various ages and nationalities. Old Oxfam, Christian Aid and Traidcraft calendars are a good source of appropriate pictures.

As babies play with the cube and look at the pictures, tell them today's Bible verses.

Mark Bible verses Use coloured paper to make markers for the Bible. Use the three verses for today as well as one or two of the general verses for this unit. At the top of each marker glue a picture of a person. Write one verse on each marker and place them at the correct place in the Bible.

Help babies to handle the Bible carefully. Read the different verses to them.

Toddlers

As with the babies, use Bible markers with pictures of people on them for toddlers today.

Give the baby doll a bath Borrow a baby bath if you can. Otherwise, a washing-up bowl will be all right. Put a few centimetres of water in it. Bring a towel and a small flannel or sponge. Cover the area around the 'bath' with newspaper to absorb spills. Let toddlers help to wash the doll. One with a plastic body and no hair is best – water drips everywhere from a doll with hair.

The doll will probably get washed more than once, but that's fine. As you work with the children on this, you can talk about them having a bath, and about how God made people.

Make a mural of people Provide a large, long strip of paper for children to work together to make a mural. Cut out pictures of people of different ages and nationalities for the children to glue on the mural. Across the top write, 'God made people'.

BIBLE STUFF — God made our world/God gives us friends

week 4

Let the children glue the pictures where they want. Don't worry if they are upside down, sideways or overlapping. Rather than being concerned with the aesthetic effect of the mural, take the opportunity to tell the children the Bible story. At the end of the session you may want to put the mural outside the room so parents can see it when they collect their children.

Play with playdough If you have playdough already made up, check that it is still fit for use. Sometimes home-made playdough goes a bit sticky after a while. Make a fresh batch if you're in doubt.

Let the children pound, squeeze and roll the dough with their hands. If you think they may want something to pound the dough with, put a few wooden bricks on the table or tray with the dough. This activity is particularly linked with today's theme – but playdough is always good fun! As the children squeeze and pound the dough you may be able to tell part of the Bible story or sing to them about God making people. Use the chorus tune of 'Jesus loves me' and sing 'God made people (x3) and he loves everyone!'

2s - 3s

Make a mural of people. Provide plenty of pictures for them to glue. Let the children play with playdough today, as well. You may want to provide some dough cutters shaped like people. If not, put out a few rolling pins or some wooden bricks for pounding the dough.

Play with stand-up figures in the brick area Make some stand-up figures of people for the brick area. Cut out four to six full-length pictures of people (children, adults and grandparents) from catalogues or magazines. Glue each picture onto some card, then cut it out. Make the people stand by attaching each picture to a cardboard tube, such as one from a kitchen towel. Place the people with the bricks.

As children play with the people, tell them about God making Adam and Eve.

Pictures of people For this activity you will need two identical magazines or catalogues. (It isn't too difficult to get two identical magazines – lots of shops have free magazines or catalogues. Pick up two copies from time to time when you are out shopping. They come in handy!)

Cut out ten or twelve sets of matching pictures of people – if possible of varying ages and races. Glue them onto individual squares of paper or card of all the same colour. Mix the cards up then spread them out on the floor and let children pair them up.

Alternatively, you can lay one set out on the floor and keep the other set in a pile. Let children take turns taking one off the pile and finding the picture that matches it.

3s - 5s

Make stand-up figures for the brick area today. Make a mural of people, or let children make their own collages of people to take home. On either write, 'God made people'.

You can also use the matching people cards as suggested for the twos and threes. If you have some more mature children in your group, you could make the game a bit harder by placing all the cards face down and letting them turn over two at a time until they can match up pairs. If you do this, start with only about six pairs, then add more if they are good at it. Vary the way you play the game according to which children are interested at the moment. Some will be quite happy just to look at the pictures and match them up. Others will enjoy a slightly greater challenge.

Look at books about people from around the world You may need to visit the children's section of the library for this activity. Books with photographs of the people and cultures of various parts of the world are what you need. Check the pictures carefully to make sure there aren't any that might distress some of the children, such as pictures of unusual rituals, or faces painted in frightening ways. If in doubt, ask.

BIBLE STUFF *God made our world/God gives us friends*

week 4

Librarians are usually more than willing to help.

As children look at the pictures you can talk about how people are different, but that God made us all and that he loves all people.

Make Bible markers Make several Bible markers, choosing several verses from all the weeks of this unit. Draw or glue pictures at the top of the markers – a sun, a tree, some flowers, animals and people. If you want to you can make it into a matching game of some kind, but the children might enjoy just choosing the different pictures at the top of the markers and having you read the verse to them. This should allow for natural conversation reinforcing all the stories of this unit.

Group Time

2s - 3s

If you have enough matching cards, you could give one to each child. Ask them all to stand together away from the group time area. Keep the set of matching pictures yourself. Hold up a picture. The child who has its pair can come to the circle and so on until all children are seated. Collect the cards from them as they come to the circle.

You might want to tell the Bible story as soon as children are settled – or it may take a song or two for that. After you have told it, you can talk with the children about how they are all different. Have them look at each other's hair. Have two children stand together and compare height. Talk about the things that are the same about people (we all have hands, feet and eyes) as well as the things that are different.

Emphasize that God made all people. Each of us is different, yet God loves each one. If any of the children want to pray, let them take turns.

As you wait for parents to come, you can play variations of the matching pictures game.

3s - 5s

Again, you may want to use the same ideas as suggested for today's twos and threes' group time. If you have a large group of children you could hand out the people cards so that children have matching pairs. Call children to the circle by name, then let them show their cards. The child who has the matching card can sit down next. Call another child and so on until all are seated.

At the end you may want to get out the books of people of different cultures and let the children look at them in small groups as they wait for parents.

BIBLE STUFF   God made our world/God gives us friends   **22**

GOD MADE OUR WORLD — WEEK 4

Take Home!

GOD MADE PEOPLE (GENESIS 1:26-31; 2:15-25)

Aim
To help the children understand that God made people and that God loves people.

Bible verses
God loves people. (John 3:16)
God made a man and a woman. (Genesis 1:27)
God knows all about everybody. (Luke 12:7)

The story
God had made the world. It was beautiful. There were lakes and rivers. There were trees and plants. There were lots of animals. But there were no people.

So God made a man. His name was Adam. God brought all the animals to Adam so he could decide what to call them.

But Adam was the only person. God did not want Adam to be alone, so he made a woman. Her name was Eve. Adam and Eve lived together in the beautiful world God had made.

There were fruit trees and vegetable plants for Adam and Eve to eat.

God told them, 'I want you to be happy in the world I have made. You will have children. The animals will have babies. You can all live together in the world I have made.'

God looked at everything he had made. He looked at the people he had made. God was very pleased.

Activity suggestions

Look at Bible verses
Use coloured paper or card to make Bible markers. Write one of the Bible verses for this week on each marker. Place them in your Bible at the correct reference. In a quiet moment (if there ever is one!) hold your baby on your lap with the Bible. Read the Bible verses aloud. As your baby hears you say, 'The Bible says...' he or she begins to understand that it is a special book.

Older under fives enjoy listening to Bible verses as well. Let them choose the marker they want, then read the verse to them.

Make a life-sized picture of your child
Find some large sheets of paper and tape several together. (Newspaper will do fine if you don't have any plain paper.) Let your child lie down on the paper, then draw his or her outline. Cut it out, then let your child colour it in. Don't worry if he or she draws clothes or features, or uses unusual colours. For young children the enjoyment is more in the doing than in the finished product.

BIBLE STUFF — *God made our world/God gives us friends*

God Made Our World — Week 5

GOD MADE ME (PSALM 139:1-16)

Aim To help the children understand that God made them, knows all about them and loves them.

Preparation

Read Psalm 139 slowly and carefully, perhaps in more than one translation. As you meditate on it, allow God to speak to you. Some of us may find the words of the psalm challenging. Others of us may be in need at this time, and will find comfort in the assurance of God's intimate knowledge of us. One of the amazing things about the Bible is that the same words can be read by all of us, but God applies them to us as individuals. Wherever we are spiritually, whatever our present circumstances, God longs to speak to us through his Word. Try to take at least fifteen minutes to be quiet before God as you read this passage. As you begin, ask him to speak to you.

'*Lord as we finish this unit on creation, I pray that the children I teach will have learned much. And I pray for myself, that I may have an even greater appreciation of all that you have made. Especially today, I pray for a new experience of you as I contemplate how completely you know me. Amen.*'

Story Time

Bible verses
God made me. (Psalm 139:13)
God knows everything about me. (Psalm 139:1)
God cares about you. (1 Peter 5:7)

Birth - 2s

A man named David wrote some words to God. Those words are in the Bible. David said: 'God, you are very wonderful. You made me. Even when I wasn't born, you knew all about me.

'You made me with arms and legs. You gave me hands and feet. You made my eyes and my ears, my nose and my mouth.

'Thank you, God, for making me. You know everything about me. Thank you, God, that you will always love me. Wherever I go, you will always be there to love me.

'It is hard for me to understand. But thank you, God, that you made me.'

3s - 5s

A man named David wrote some words to God. Those words are in the Bible. David said: 'God, you are very wonderful. You made me. Even before I was born you knew all about me.

'You knew what I would look like. You gave me arms and legs. You made me with hands and feet. God, you gave me eyes and ears, a nose and a mouth. It is wonderful to know that you made me.

'Thank you, God, for making me. You know everything about me. You know the things I am going to do and say. Thank you, God, that you will always love me.

'You love me when I am awake. You love me even when I am asleep. God, I know that wherever I go you will always be there to love me.

'It is hard for me to understand. But thank you, God, that you made me.'

BIBLE STUFF *God made our world/God gives us friends*

Week 5

Teaching Activities

What an amazing thing it is to know that God knew us even as we were growing in our mother's womb! How incredible that he knew how long we would live before we were even born! Sometimes God's intimate knowledge of us is threatening because we have things we want to hide from him. Let's clear all that away before we teach today. As God has spoken to us through his word, so we have a living faith to pass on – a faith that hopefully has grown even this week.

Psalm 139 says we are beautifully and wonderfully made. As we teach today, let's communicate that sense of wonder at how God has made our bodies.

Babies

Make a book of textures Find four or five items with different textures to make a book. Mount each one on a separate piece of card. Cotton wool, sandpaper, velvet, plastic 'bubble pack' packing material and corrugated cardboard are the kinds of things you could use. If using cotton wool, take care that babies don't pull it off the page and put it in their mouths.

As babies feel the different textures, talk to them about their hands and about being able to touch and feel. Thank God for hands and fingers.

Listen to bells If your church has a supply of children's musical instruments there may well be some bells or some other instruments (perhaps a triangle or tambourine) which make a pleasant ringing type of sound. Let older babies shake them. You can make the sounds for younger babies. As they turn their heads to the sound, thank God for ears to hear.

Look in a mirror This activity was suggested last week, but it is certainly appropriate again today. As a baby looks in the mirror say to her: 'God made you. Thank you, God, for Sarah. Thank you for giving Sarah eyes to see.'

Water play Put a few centimetres of water in a washing-up bowl and let babies splash their fingers in it. If it is a warm day and some of them are barefoot, they could even splash their toes. Bring one or two towels for drying hands and feet.

As babies enjoy the water, tell them about God making them. Tell them about David's words in Psalm 139.

Toddlers

Make a texture book for toddlers as suggested for babies.

Follow a footprint path Cut out lots of child-sized footprints and stick them on the floor to make a path around the room. Make sure that they are close enough together for toddler-sized steps! As children follow the winding path around the room, thank God for legs and feet to walk.

Make 'God made me' pictures Ask around in your church to see if someone has a Polaroid 'instant picture' camera. Film for these cameras is expensive, but this is a special treat.

Take a picture of each child and let him or her watch as it develops. This is great fun for adults and children. Be careful that the children don't touch the picture while it is developing. Resist the temptation to call it magic - it isn't. It's very clever, but it isn't magic!

BIBLE STUFF   *God made our world/God gives us friends*

Week 5

You will need some lightweight card onto which you can mount each photograph. Let the children colour on their pieces of card with crayons or coloured pencils, then glue the picture on the card. Make sure they do the colouring first, otherwise they will probably draw over the picture. At the top or the bottom write: 'God made me'. As children make these pictures, tell them the Bible story for today.

If this activity is not possible for you, let the children have chunky crayons to colour on the body shapes (as suggested in following sections). They will only be able to scribble but that is fine ñ they will enjoy the act of colouring.

Water play or water painting Your choice of activities will depend on the weather. If it is warm and dry you can go outside and paint with water. You may want to take children out two at a time. Each child needs a clean paintbrush and a spill-proof paint container with water in it. Let them 'paint' the path, the wall, pillars, posts – just about anything. Even if they spill or drip on their clothes, it is only water.

If the weather isn't great, have water play inside, with a few plastic cups and sieves in the water to play with. As children enjoy either activity, tell them today's Bible verses.

2s - 3s

Make a 'feel bag' Adapt the 'texture book' as follows. Prepare two samples of each of the items suggested for the book – or of other textured items that you can find. Put them all in a cloth bag or some other bag that the children can't easily see into. Let the children reach in and pull out one item. Let them look at it and feel it, then place it to one side. Let them put their hand in the bag again and see if they can find the matching item. If this is too difficult for some two-year-olds, they will just enjoy putting their hand in the bag and feeling the items.

Paint on outlines of bodies Draw a set of simple body outlines about forty-five centimetres high. Cut out enough to let each child have one. Provide one or two colours of paint and let the children paint on the body outlines. They can do this at a table or an easel, whichever suits you.

Most children this age won't paint any recognizable features. That is fine. They can paint whatever they want. As they paint, draw their attention to the shape of the paper, and talk with them about how God made them.

Match sounds of shakers Make four matching pairs of shakers. Empty film canisters work well for this. If you do not have any, you may be able to get some from a chemist or a film-processing shop. In one set put a spoonful of salt, in another a small amount of rice or lentils. In the third put some pasta broken up small enough to rattle well, and in the fourth put two pennies. These four will make quite distinct sounds. Make sure that the containers are securely sealed.

Put the shakers together and let children try to find the sounds which match. Again, for some children this may be difficult, but they can enjoy listening to the sounds anyway. Thank God for ears to hear. Talk with them about other things they can hear.

Go for a looking and listening walk

Of course this activity depends on the weather. But if it is fine, take the children outside for a walk to see what they can see and to hear what they can hear. You may not think that the area surrounding the place where you meet is very interesting, but two and three-year-olds are much easier to please than adults! The emphasis of this activity is on ears and eyes and thanking God for making us, not on the scenic beauty of, say, your church car park!

It doesn't really matter whether you take all the children out together or just two or three at a time. Do whatever suits your situation the best. If the weather is against you, repeat the matching stars activity from Week 1.

BIBLE STUFF *God made our world/God gives us friends*

Week 5

3s - 5s

Matching textures in a feel bag will be fun for the threes to fives today. Cut out outlines of bodies for them as well, but let them colour rather than paint. Washable felt tips and crayons are both suitable. Many children will draw faces, some will draw clothes. Try to let them do their own work and don't make them feel they have to colour a certain way. Purple hair and orange eyes are not a problem for children of this age!

While the children are involved in both of these activities, conversation about how wonderfully God has made us may flow easily. You could even tell the children that the Bible says 'I am wonderfully made'.

Match smells Make four or five pairs of matching smells. You can use old film canisters for this. Place a bit of cotton wool inside each one to absorb the smell. It is probably a good idea to prepare them as close as possible to the time when they are to be used – the day before will be all right if you keep the lids on them. Lemon juice, cinnamon or mixed spice, curry powder, chocolate, onion or garlic powder, vanilla essence, perfume and after shave are all possibilities. Use what you have. Don't forget to make up two containers for each smell.

Just before the session pierce the lids of the containers so the children can smell without seeing. Let them try to match up the smells. If it is too difficult for them, just let them sniff and talk about each smell. Thank God for noses to smell things.

Tape record the children's voices Bring a portable tape recorder with you. As one or two children approach you, switch on and record thirty seconds of conversation. Play it back to them. Most children are very intrigued by this. They may be used to video cameras, but not many will be used to hearing their voice on cassette. Let them take turns singing a song, or saying a Bible verse, and then listening to the play-back. Thank God not only for ears, but also for voices.

Give the baby doll a bath This idea was suggested for toddlers last week and for twos and threes in Week 1 of this unit. Some of the children might have baby brothers or sisters, so this will be a common activity in their house (with a real baby, not a doll, of course!). As you work together to wash the doll, tell the children today's Bible story.

Group Time

2s - 3s

Start group time with songs or movements that emphasize different parts of the body. Do actions that involve standing up and sitting down. This should 'get the wiggles out' so the children can sit quietly while you tell the Bible story. Talk about the different parts of their bodies that they used during the session in various activities. If any children want to pray, let them do so. It could be as simple as 'Thank you, God, for making me'.

As you wait for parents to arrive you could play a simple 'follow the leader' game as you lead the children around the room. Remember that most children of this age can't skip yet, and only some can hop. But they can wave their arms and stamp their feet.

3s - 5s

You can use the same ideas as suggested for today's group time for twos and threes. In actions, movement and 'follow the leader' change the body movements to reflect the maturity of your group.

BIBLE STUFF — *God made our world/God gives us friends*

GOD MADE OUR WORLD — WEEK 5

Take Home!

GOD MADE ME (PSALM 139:1-16)

Aim To help the children understand that God made them; that God knows all about them and that he loves them.

Bible verses
God made me. (Psalm 139:13)
God knows everything about me. (Psalm 139:1)
God cares about you. (1 Peter 5:7)

The story
A man named David wrote some words to God. Those words are in the Bible. David said: 'God, you are very wonderful. You made me. Even before I was born you knew all about me.

'You knew what I would look like. You gave me arms and legs. You made me with hands and feet. God, you gave me eyes and ears, a nose and a mouth. It is wonderful to know that you made me.

'Thank you, God, for making me. You know everything about me. You know the things I am going to do and say. Thank you, God, that you will always love me.

'You love me when I am awake. You love me even when I am asleep. God, I know that wherever I go you will always be there to love me.

'It is hard for me to understand. But thank you, God, that you made me.'

Activity suggestions

Feel different textures
Gather together several different textures for your baby to feel. Talk about rough and smooth. Let him or her feel fabrics, cotton wool, textures of different fruits and vegetables. You may want to take your baby outside to feel bricks, grass, tree bark, etc. Tell this week's Bible story.

Older under fives will also enjoy this activity.

Go for a looking and listening walk
Take a special walk when you are not in a hurry. Tell your child that you are looking to see what you can see, and listening to hear what you can hear. You may be surprised at how much your child notices. Remember that even small things are interesting to a young child.

Remember to thank God for giving us eyes and ears.

God Gives Us Friends   Week 1

DAVID AND JONATHAN (1 SAMUEL 18:1-4; 19:1-7; 2 SAMUEL 9)

Aim To help the children understand that friendships can last a long time; that friends look after each other.

Preparation

The friendship of David and Jonathan is one of lifelong loyalty and commitment. David comes to live at the palace with King Saul. He is an up-and-coming young warrior, and he also plays the harp to soothe Saul's anguished mind. Saul's son, Jonathan, takes a shine to David. In fact, the Bible tells us that 'he loved him as himself', or in some of the older translations, 'as his own soul'.

David and Jonathan declared a lifelong loyalty and commitment to one another. This loyalty extended even beyond death (2 Samuel 9). Their friendship stood the test of many stresses and pressures. When Saul wanted to take David's life, Jonathan did not want to have anything to do with it. He warned David, then stepped in as peacemaker. He was certainly caught in the middle in that situation.

As we use David and Jonathan's friendship to teach the children about friends, let's learn from it ourselves. No friendship is ever free from complications. Some friendships seem to undergo serious testing and turbulence. But God calls us to demonstrate a quality of friendship that remains loyal, that keeps loving and goes on caring even when it is difficult. God has called us his friends and he wants us to love others with the same love that he loves us. May we be filled with that love so it can spill over onto our friends – and to the children we teach!

'*As I prepare to teach today, Lord, help me to think of those people who have been my friends for a long time, or those who have shown loyalty and care for me and my family. Thank you Lord, for the gift of friendship. Thank you that the most important example of this is you – you have called me your friend. What a privilege! Amen.*'

Story Time

Bible verses
David and Jonathan were good friends. (1 Samuel 18:1)
David and Jonathan promised to be friends always. (1 Samuel 18:3)
A friend loves at all times. (Proverbs 17:17)

Birth - 2s
David was one of King Saul's helpers. He lived at the king's palace. King Saul had a son named Jonathan. David and Jonathan were good friends.

One day Jonathan said to David: 'You are my special friend. We will always be friends.' Then Jonathan gave David his own coat, his belt and his bow and arrows. Jonathan wanted to show David how much he loved him.

When a man wanted to hurt David, Jonathan talked to the man. He asked the man not to hurt David.

Many years later David was kind to Jonathan's son. David and Jonathan were good friends. They looked after each other. They were always friends.

3s - 5s

David was one of King Saul's helpers. He lived at the king's palace. King Saul had a son named Jonathan. David and Jonathan became good friends. They loved each other very much.

One day Jonathan said to David: 'You are my special friend. Let's promise that we will always be friends.' Jonathan gave David a present to show that they would always be friends. He gave David his own coat, his belt and his bow and arrows. Giving David a present was Jonathan's way of showing David how much he loved him.

When a man wanted to hurt David, Jonathan went to talk to the man. He asked the man not to hurt David.

Many years later David was kind to Jonathan's son. He made sure that Jonathan's son would always have enough money and enough food to eat.

David and Jonathan were good friends. They helped each other. They loved each other. They were always friends.

Teaching Activities

We want to emphasize David and Jonathan's friendship. That is why in the story we say only that 'a man' wanted to hurt David. Naming him as King Saul could raise many questions about why the king would want to hurt one of his helpers. The Bible is strong enough to take all our questions, but children's questions in this case would be hard to answer, and could certainly lead to an awkward group time. We need to keep on asking God for wisdom as we try to teach the Bible in ways that under fives can relate to and understand.

Babies

Sing songs about friends Because simple yet meaningful songs for under fives are hard to find, you will need to make up some of your own to go with every unit of teaching. Only a few phrases are necessary, and it is perfectly acceptable to use well known tunes if you don't want to make up your own. Words such as 'Thank you God for friends', 'David and Jonathan were friends' (changing the names for each week's story), and 'Friends help each other' are all suitable.

Make a book of friends Cut out several pictures of different age groups of people: babies, children, teenagers and adults. Also try to find one or two pictures of mixed age groups. Glue them on pieces of card. Punch holes along the left-hand side, then tie them together with ribbon or wool. On the front write: 'Thank you, God, for friends'. As you show babies the pictures, tell them about David and Jonathan.

Blow bubbles Children are usually fascinated by bubbles. Just a simple bottle of bubble solution is fine – you don't need any fancy bubble blowers. You can even blow bubbles over the buggy or pram of a young baby. Do be careful – sometimes when the bubbles burst the solution drops everywhere. Make sure it doesn't pop in a baby's face. As babies watch the bubbles you can thank God for eyes to see and for friends at church.

Play with a beach ball Blow up a plastic beach ball and let babies roll it around. It may even be possible for you to throw it gently to some babies. Even young babies who are out of their prams and lying on the floor will probably watch a colourful beach ball roll around. You may want to sing songs about friends as you roll the ball.

Week 1

Toddlers

Make a book about friends for toddlers to look at, and sing songs about friends. Blow bubbles, as well, though you may want to save that until the end of the session. Children tend to get excited chasing bubbles. You could use bubbles as you wait for parents to arrive.

Sand play Provide cups, a funnel and one or two sieves with the sand today. You may need to limit how many children can do this activity at one time according to the size of your sand container. No more than three will fit round a washing-up bowl; probably four could manage around a baby bath. If you have a proper sand-play table, there might be room for more. Make sure that there is at least one play item (cup, sieve or funnel) per child. You can help them take turns with them. As children play, you can talk about fun things we do with friends. You can tell part of the story of David and Jonathan.

Make a collage of friends Cut pictures from catalogues and magazines of people together. Let children choose pictures to glue on their own piece of paper. When they have finished, try to find a space to write: 'Thank you, God, for friends'. Let the children glue as much as they can by themselves. The children gain more by doing their own work than by having a 'beautiful' picture to look at afterwards. As children make their collages tell them about David and Jonathan's friendship.

2s - 3s

Use songs about friends with twos and threes today. For example, use the tune of the first two lines of 'Old MacDonald' and sing: 'Thank you, God, for giving us friends'. Or, make up a very simple tune for the words: 'I have a good friend... is her/his name.' Sing the child's name to him or her. Try making collage pictures of friends.

Sort items by colour Use coloured beads or cotton reels for sorting. Smaller coloured beads are fine, as long as they are not too small for little hands to manage. Put the items to be sorted into a container. As the children take them out, they can make separate piles for each colour.

Six colours is about the maximum number that children of this age can sort. If you don't have beads or cotton reels, you could use coloured clothes pegs instead. As children work to sort beads you may be able to tell part of the Bible story, or talk to them about how they are working with their friends to sort the beads.

Peg clothes on a 'washing line' Find a way to make a washing line in your classroom. You may be able to tie some string to the backs of two chairs. The line should be very low so that children can reach it. Bring some clothes and pegs and a washing basket. Some children won't be able to manage pegs, but they can still lay the clothes over the line. Socks are good for this. Don't bring large adult items because they will be too big and awkward for most children to handle.

As you help children and as they help one another, you can talk or sing about friends and say thank you to God for them.

Make instant whip Make a sign for the door announcing that you will be making instant whip and asking parents to alert you to any allergies that may affect their child. Bring all the things necessary to make instant whip – choose sugar-free vanilla or strawberry flavour. It is better to avoid chocolate as some children may be allergic to it – and it is messier! One packet will make enough for eight children. Bring milk and a measuring jug. Let the children all have a turn at pouring a bit of the instant whip powder into the mixing bowl, or pouring in some of the milk. Try to let everyone who wants to have a turn with the rotary beater or whisk.

Bring plastic cups and a spoon for each child. Spoon a small amount of instant whip into each cup and let the children eat it straight away. This activity will probably interest every child, even if they don't like instant whip! You may find yourself surrounded by all the children at once. When you have finished, they can return to the other activities.

As you supervise children pouring or mixing you might want to sing songs about friends or tell part of the story so that you keep the attention of the children who are waiting their turn.

Week 1

3s - 5s

Songs are always appropriate for any age group of under fives, so make up some songs about friends to use in this unit. Pegging clothes on the washing line and making instant whip are two activities you can use today.

Draw with chalks If you do not already have a set, purchase a small box of children's coloured drawing chalks. You may want to let the children draw on black or dark-coloured paper today. Chalks tend to be more effective against a dark background. You may need to have a bowl of water for washing hands, or at least a wet cloth as chalk dust can get all over hands and arms. It may be as well to put painting aprons over the children's clothes, too.

If you are able to chat with children as they work, you can talk to them about their friends at church, play group or nursery, and you can tell them about David and Jonathan.

Make a friends booklet Let the children help you make a booklet of friends. This can be done in one of two ways. If you have access to a Polaroid camera (and if your budget will allow the purchase of a film for it), take pictures of the children. You may want to take two or three children together to make the film go further. Make sure the teachers are included in the photos. Children will be absolutely fascinated as they watch the picture develop before their eyes. You can then glue one picture on each page of the book. On the cover write, 'Friends at Church'. On each page write the names of the children who appear in the picture.

Alternatively, provide several pictures of people together. Let a child choose a picture to glue on a page of the book, then let him or her use crayons or felt tips to 'decorate' the page as well. You may want to ask the children who their friends are and what they like to do with their friends. You could then write a sentence on their page like 'John's friend is Michael' or 'John likes to play cars with his friends'. When every child who wants to has made a page for the book, punch holes along the left-hand side and tie the pages together with ribbon or wool. Use plain paper for the cover and write 'Thank you, God, for friends' on it.

Play with playdough Provide playdough, rolling pins and some pastry shapes for children to play with. Let the children do this activity in the home corner, or in an area separate from the main part of the room. Talk with the children about friends as they play, or sing songs about friendship.

Group Time

2s - 3s

You could start group time today by singing to each child in turn round the circle: 'I have a good friend, … is his/her name.' When you have sung every child's name and the name of other teachers in the circle, say: 'Thank you, God, for friends.' After you tell the story, children might be ready for conversation as you ask: 'What did you do with your friends here today?' You can blow bubbles while you are waiting for parents to arrive.

3s - 5s

You can use the song suggested for twos and threes to start group time. You can also sing some of the songs you have made up about friends. If you sing them every week in this unit, the children will begin to know them and sing along with you. When the children have settled enough to listen, tell the Bible story. Give any children who want to an opportunity to pray. Encourage the children in conversation about friends.

Show the book that was made earlier in the session. Children will be keen to say, 'That's my page'. You can probably keep looking at the book as parents are arriving, but if you need something else, threes to fives will enjoy bubbles just as much as the younger children.

BIBLE STUFF *God made our world/God gives us friends*

GOD GIVES US FRIENDS — WEEK 1

Take Home!

DAVID AND JONATHAN (1 SAMUEL 18:1-4; 19:1-7; 2 SAMUEL 9)

Aim
To help the children understand that friendships can last a long time; that friends look after each other.

Bible verses
David and Jonathan were good friends.
(1 Samuel 18:1)
David and Jonathan promised to be friends always.
(1 Samuel 18:3)
A friend loves at all times. (Proverbs 17:17)

The story
David was one of King Saul's helpers. He lived at the king's palace. King Saul had a son named Jonathan. David and Jonathan became good friends. They loved each other very much.

One day Jonathan said to David: 'You are my special friend. Let's promise that we will always be friends.' Jonathan gave David a present to show that they would always be friends. He gave David his own coat, his belt and his bow and arrows. Giving David a present was Jonathan's way of showing David how much he loved him.

When a man wanted to hurt David, Jonathan went to talk to the man. He asked the man not to hurt David.

Many years later David was kind to Jonathan's son. He made sure that Jonathan's son would always have enough money and enough food to eat.

David and Jonathan were good friends. They helped each other. They loved each other. They were always friends.

Activity suggestions
Blow bubbles
You will need a small bottle of bubble solution. Blow bubbles for your baby to watch – or for your child to chase. As you do this, tell the story of David and Jonathan. Talk to your baby or child about their friends. Say thank you to God for friends.

Make a child-sized washing line
Use some string to make a very low washing line at home. Let your child lay socks or small garments over the line. Use pegs if he or she can manage them. Most children enjoy doing 'grownup' things. This activity is not necessarily related to the theme of friends, but it is a fun, developmental activity to share. Doing things like this together gives you time to be with your child. Often, it provides natural opportunities for the sharing of the Bible story or Bible verses.

BIBLE STUFF — *God made our world/God gives us friends*

God Gives Us Friends   Week 2

FOUR FRIENDS (MARK 2:1-12; LUKE 5:17-26)

Aim To help the children learn that friends help each other – they do things for one another.

Preparation

Last week we looked at lifelong loyalty and commitment. Today, we look at God's intention that we help one another, even when it isn't convenient, even when it is a bit messy.

Look at the four friends. The Bible says that Jesus acted when he saw their faith. We do not know whether the paralysed man had any faith that Jesus could heal him. We don't even know whether he went to see Jesus willingly, or whether his friends just took him because they believed. When their original plan didn't work (i.e. going in the front door) they didn't give up and say: 'I guess it just wasn't meant to be.' No, they weren't put off by barriers. They came up with Plan B.

What an encouragement to know that God can work through our faith to move in the lives of others. What's more, in those times when our own faith is running low, we can still see God at work when our friends have faith, and they pray for his power to be at work in our lives.

The concept of Jesus acting in response to the faith of the friends is beyond the understanding of under fives. What we can teach them from this story is that the four men knew Jesus could make their friend well. They wanted to help their friend, so they took him to Jesus.

'*Father, as I prepare for today, help me to think of my adult friends and how I can bring them to Jesus. Help me also to think of the children as my friends. Help me to bring them to Jesus this week by praying for them and by demonstrating his love and compassion. Thank you for the opportunity to influence young lives for Jesus' sake. Amen.*'

Story Time

Bible verses
Four men brought their friend to see Jesus. (Mark 2:3)
The men knew that Jesus could make their friend well. (Luke 5:19-20)
Jesus made a man well. (Mark 2:12)
A friend loves at all times. (Proverbs 17:17)

Birth - 2s
One day the people came to hear Jesus teach about God. The house where he was staying was full of people. There was no room for anybody else.

Four men brought their friend to see Jesus. They had to carry him on a mat because he could not walk. The four men knew that Jesus could make their friend well.

There were so many people that the men and their friend couldn't get to Jesus. So they went up the stairs on the outside of the house and climbed onto the flat roof. They took away part of the roof so they could let their friend down through the hole.

When Jesus saw the man and his friends, he made the man well. Now the man could walk. He was very happy. The four men had helped their friend. They had taken him to see Jesus.

Week 2

3s - 5s

Wherever Jesus went, lots of people wanted to see him. Jesus taught the people about God and he made sick people well. One day, many people came to hear Jesus teach. The house where he was staying was so full of people that they were standing in the doorway and even outside. There was no room for anybody else.

Four men brought their friend to see Jesus. They had to carry him on a mat because he could not walk. The four men knew that Jesus could make their friend well.

There were so many people that the men and their friend couldn't get to Jesus. So they went up the stairs on the outside of the house and onto the flat roof. They took away part of the roof so they could let their friend down through the hole.

When Jesus saw the man and his friends he said to the man, 'God knows that you are sorry for the wrong things you have done. You can get up and walk now because you are well.'

The man got up and he could walk. Jesus had made him well. He was very happy.

The four men had helped their friend. They had taken him to see Jesus.

Teaching Activities

As always, our concern is to provide fun and meaningful activities for the children, and to teach them the things of God as we do those activities. Let's pray that through this unit on friends we may be able to build some strong foundations for healthy friendships as the children grow.

Babies

Make a toy from bells and ribbons Find some scraps of ribbon (not more than fifteen centimetres long) and a few small bells. If you have bells in your collection of musical instruments, you may be able to detach these and use them. Tie a bell securely to one end of a piece of ribbon. Thread the other end of the ribbon through the hole of a large button, or a wooden ring of some kind. How many pieces of ribbon you attach to the toy depends on what you are using to keep them together – a button may have two or four holes, a wooden ring could hold a number of ribbons, but four is probably enough. Make sure that babies don't try to put the bells into their mouths.

As you shake the toy for younger babies, or as older ones shake it themselves, thank God for ears to hear.

Touch and look at hard fruits Bring some hard fruits in a basket for babies to handle. A small melon, an apple, an orange and a firm kiwi fruit would all be tough enough. Let the babies feel the different textures and see the different colours of the fruit. As the babies play with the fruits, tell them about the four men and their friend.

Keep a balloon in the air Blow up one or two brightly coloured balloons. Bounce the balloon off your hands and keep it in the air. Even a young baby in a pram will watch the movement of the balloon. Older babies will also enjoy watching. Whether or not you let the babies play with the balloons depends on how closely you can supervise them, and whether you are willing to take the risk of a balloon bursting and frightening the babies.

As you 'float' a balloon for a baby, call him by name: 'Benjamin, you are my friend. I'm glad you are my friend,' or 'I'm glad God gives us friends.'

week 2

Toddlers

Toddlers will enjoy 'floating' a balloon, but be careful not to let them become over-excited with this activity. You may want to have balloons out two or three times during the session for only a few minutes each time. Bring fruits to look at as well. You can let the children taste the apple. Make sure you remove the peel as many children this age can't chew the peel and they could easily choke.

Paint at the easel One colour is enough for toddlers. Cover the floor under the easel with newspaper. Provide aprons to protect children's clothing. Even if you have a double-sided easel, you will probably find that you can only supervise one toddler at a time. Guide a child to wipe the brush against the side of the paint pot before putting it to the paper. This helps to avoid some drips. You will need to have a bowl of warm, soapy water for washing hands.

As the children paint, sing to them about the friends in the story. As always, use only a few simple words. Try making up a tune to go with, 'Four men took their friend to Jesus; Jesus made him well.' (You can also fit these words to the tune of 'London Bridge is falling down'.)

Play with playdough You might want to provide a few wooden bricks to pound or squash the dough with. Toddlers can manage these. They sometimes become frustrated with rolling pins and shape cutters because they can't use them without help.

2s - 3s

Provide playdough for the twos and threes today. Some children of this age will be able to roll the dough. They will also enjoy pounding the dough with wooden bricks. Some of the following group activities are drawn from those used last week by other groups.

Sand play As with toddlers last week, put cups, funnels and sieves with the sand. As children play, remind them to take turns with these items. You could say: 'The Bible says be kind to one another. You are being kind when you let Jennifer have her turn. It will be your turn in a minute.'

Draw with chalks As with threes to fives last week, use dark-coloured paper for greater effect with chalks. Some children of this age may not have used chalks before and may need guidance in holding and using them gently so they don't break. As always with art activities, there are opportunities for conversation about the teaching theme, and sometimes opportunities for silence. We must ask God to make us wise about how best to teach.

Make stand-up figures of friends for the bricks Cut out four or five pictures of people together, both adults and children. Glue them to some lightweight card, then attach them to empty cardboard tubes so they will stand up. Put them with the bricks. As children play, you can use the figures to talk about friends.

Make a Bible verse marker game Make six or eight Bible markers using different colours of paper. Write a different verse on each marker, choosing from the verses used in this unit. At the top of each marker (the bit that will stick out at the top of the Bible) draw a different shape – circle, triangle, square, rectangle, diamond, star, octagon and an irregular shape are all fairly recognizable by children of this age. Cut a paper square (approximately ten centimetres) in each of the colours you used for markers. Draw shapes on the squares to correspond with those on the markers.

Place the markers at the appropriate place in the Bible, then spread the squares out on the floor. Let children choose a square, then find the matching marker. Read the Bible verse to them. Depending on the number of children sitting with you and their level of interest, you may be able to talk about the Bible story that goes with the verse, or talk about friends in general. If not, just reading the verses to children is helpful. It is good for them to hear the teacher say, 'The Bible says…'.

week 2

3s - 5s

Use sand play with the threes to fives today, as well as the stand-up figures with the bricks and the Bible marker game. You may also want to try some of the following activities.

Sort beads This activity was suggested last week for the twos and threes. You can use it in the same way. Depending on what items you are sorting, and how many colours you have available, threes to fives could manage as many as eight colours. As two children work together, you can talk to them about friends taking turns, and friends helping each other.

Play with a doctor's kit Use an empty plastic container with a lid (an old ice cream carton works well) to make a doctor's kit. If you have any empty plastic medicine bottles, put one or two in. Do not put sweets in bottles as pretend tablets. This could lead to children taking real tablets at home, thinking they are sweets. Try to find an old stretch bandage or a long wrapping bandage; you may need to cut it in half to make two bandages of manageable length. You can make pretend plasters by cutting short strips of masking tape and putting a square of paper in the middle of each piece. For children to use, stick them to something from which they can be peeled. An enjoyable optional extra would be to let the children try using a stethoscope.

The children may want to use a doll as the 'patient', or even the teacher! Some children are happy to have a plaster or bandage put on them, others are very reluctant. Let each child do what they feel comfortable with. As the children play 'doctor', talk with them about how the doctor helps to make us well, and about how Jesus made a man well.

Make a collage of friends Cut out some pictures of people in pairs or groups. If you have time to supervise them, allow the children to cut out their own pictures from old magazine or catalogue pages. Let each child make his or her own collage. When they have finished gluing their pictures write 'Thank you, God, for friends' on each paper.

As they work you can talk about their friends, and about the four friends who brought a man to Jesus.

Group Time

2s - 3s

When the children come to group time from all the activities of the session, it will take a minute or two before they are settled enough to listen to the Bible story. Use that time to chat about the activities they have participated in, sing songs, or do movement rhymes. When you want to tell the story, say something like, 'Now it is my turn to talk for a minute. I want to tell you a story from the Bible.'

After the story, give children an opportunity to pray, and chat or sing some more. When it is time for parents to come, get the Bible marker game out again. Using that in a group context is good way of helping the children practise waiting their turn.

3s - 5s

At the start of group time, children need a minute or two to change gear. If they have helped tidy the room, that begins the process. They realize that now it is time to do something else.

As they come to the group, start with a song or some movements that they can all be involved in. Use music, conversation, prayer and the Bible story each week. But vary the order according to how well they are listening; be guided by your sense of when it is time to move on. As with the twos and threes, you can finish today with the Bible marker game.

GOD GIVES US FRIENDS — WEEK 2

Take Home!

FOUR FRIENDS (MARK 2:1-12; LUKE 5:17-26)

Aim
To help the children learn that friends help each other – they do things for one another.

Bible verses
Four men brought their friend to see Jesus. (Mark 2:3)
The men knew that Jesus could make their friend well. (Luke 5:19-20)
Jesus made a man well. (Mark 2:12)
A friend loves at all times. (Proverbs 17:17)

The story
Wherever Jesus went, lots of people wanted to see him. Jesus taught the people about God and he made sick people well. One day, many people came to hear Jesus teach. The house where he was staying was so full of people that they were standing in the doorway and even outside. There was no room for anybody else.

Four men brought their friend to see Jesus. They had to carry him on a mat because he could not walk. The four men knew that Jesus could make their friend well.

There were so many people that the men and their friend couldn't get to Jesus. So they went up the stairs on the outside of the house and onto the flat roof. They took away part of the roof so they could let their friend down through the hole.

When Jesus saw the man and his friends he said to the man, 'God knows that you are sorry for the wrong things you have done. You can get up and walk now because you are well.'

The man got up and he could walk. Jesus had made him well. He was very happy.

The four men had helped their friend. They had taken him to see Jesus.

Activity suggestions
Touch and look at various fruits
Give your baby the opportunity to handle a variety of different fruits. Make sure they are fairly tough – melon, apple, orange and kiwi, rather than banana or strawberries!

An older under five might enjoy watching you cut the fruits open to see what is inside. You may want to taste the fruit together.

As with last week's activities, this is one is not obviously related to the topic of friends – but it allows you and your baby or child to be friends as you share the activity. You can tell or read the Bible story in this context.

Make a card for a sick friend
Let your child draw a picture or make a card for someone you know who is not well. Deliver it in person, if possible. If not, let your child help you post it.

As you do this, talk about the men who took their friend to Jesus. Help your child to pray simply for your sick friend.

God Gives Us Friends week 3

PAUL AND TIMOTHY (ACTS 16:1-5; 2 TIMOTHY 4:9-18)

Aim To help the children learn that friends work together; that they can tell people about Jesus together; that friends don't have to be the same age.

Preparation

The relationship between Paul and Timothy was one of friendship as well as mentoring and discipling. It is a lovely picture of friendship that crosses age barriers. It is also a strong example of friends joined together in the work of the Kingdom of God.

The aspect of Paul and Timothy's relationship that we want to emphasize most is their friendship. It existed separately from the discipling and partnership, yet it affected them greatly. The first two relationships would not have been as rich and effective as they were without the friendship that Paul and Timothy enjoyed. Their friendship was a gift from God that enriched their lives.

As we meditate this week, let's think about the different relationships we have. Teaching under fives is a kind of discipling relationship. We are passing on the faith to someone else. And perhaps we are involved in other discipling relationships, within our families or within the church.

As teachers we are partners in the task of shaping the next generation for God – partners with each other and partners with the parents of the children we teach.

God has given us the gift of friendship. It is precious. We must take care of those friendships we already have, and perhaps seek to develop others. Let's ask God that our church family will be energized for the gospel by relationships of discipling and partnership. But let's also pray that our lives will be enriched by the joy of deep friendship.

'Lord, help me to sense the significance of the 'discipling' relationship I have as I teach under fives. Help me to see the children as friends also. Thank you that in your family friendship crosses not only age barriers, but all other barriers as well. Thank you for my friends. I pray in the name of my friend, Jesus. Amen.'

Story Time

Bible verses
Paul and Timothy worked together. (Acts 16:3)
Paul loved his friend Timothy. (1 Corinthians 4:17)
Paul and Timothy taught people about God. (Acts 16:4)

Birth - 2s
Paul loved Jesus. He went to lots of different towns to tell people about Jesus. One day he met a young man named Timothy. Timothy loved Jesus too.

Paul asked Timothy to go with him to tell people about Jesus. Paul and Timothy became good friends. They worked together to help people learn more about Jesus.

When they weren't in the same town, Paul wrote letters to Timothy. He told him how to teach the people. He told Timothy that he missed him.

Paul and Timothy were good friends. They liked working together to tell people about Jesus.

Week 3

3s - 5s

Paul loved Jesus. He went to lots of different towns to tell people about Jesus. He wanted to help many people love Jesus like he did. One day Paul visited a town and met a young man named Timothy. Timothy loved Jesus. A lot of people in the town knew Timothy and they liked him very much.

Paul was ready to go to some other towns. He asked Timothy to go with him to tell people about Jesus. Paul and Timothy became good friends. They worked together for many years to help people learn more about Jesus.

Sometimes Paul went to one town and Timothy went to a different town. When they weren't together, Paul wrote letters to Timothy. He told him how to teach the people. He told Timothy that he missed him. He liked it when Timothy was able to be with him.

Paul and Timothy were very good friends. They liked working together to tell people about Jesus.

 ## Teaching Activities

As we teach today we want to help the children see friendship with people of all ages as natural and happy. We also want to help them see that people working together to tell others about Jesus should be a normal part of our everyday lives.

Babies

Make markers for Bible verses Make about half a dozen bookmarks from different coloured paper. On each one write one of the Bible verses we are using in this unit. At the top of each marker glue a picture of 'friends' – people of varying ages together. Place the markers in the Bible at the appropriate reference point.

As you hold a baby on your lap, open the Bible to one of the markers and read the verse. You may want to talk to a baby about the verse, or just go on to read another one. As babies hear you say, 'The Bible says…', they begin to understand that the Bible is a special book.

Play a tape of lively music Bring a portable tape player. Choose a tape of upbeat music to play. It could be instrumental, a children's praise tape or an adult worship tape. Play it continuously, or just for short intervals if you prefer.

Make shakers Save small plastic drink bottles to make shakers. Make three or four, putting something different in each one to vary the sounds. Dry rice, pasta, lentils and other pulses are all suitable. Salt and sand make a very gentle sound. You only need a small amount to make an adequate sound. As you shake a bottle, or babies shake it themselves, be natural in saying thank you to God for ears to hear.

Sand play This activity is only suitable for older babies, and can only be done with adequate supervision. Put two or three centimetres of dry sand in a large plastic bowl. Hold a baby on your lap, or sit very close to her, and let her put her hands in the sand. You may want to sprinkle it over the baby's hands at first until she gets the idea. Some babies may not like it at all. When a baby has finished, use a dry towel to rub or brush as much sand as possible from her hands. You may want to have a small bowl of water ready in case you need to wash the sand off.

As babies play in the sand you can tell them about Paul and Timothy. When parents collect their children, be sure to mention this activity to them – then they won't wonder if they find sand in socks or shoes, or even nappies. It's amazing where even a small amount of sand can get!

Week 3

Toddlers

Make Bible verse markers for toddlers today, as well as shakers with different sounds. The following are additional activities.

Colour with crayons Provide about half a dozen colours of chunky crayons. Cut white paper into random shapes. Some toddlers will 'scribble' for about fifteen seconds, then be finished. Others will work for a few minutes with crayons. Sometimes it hardly seems worth doing, but it is part of the developmental process. Even with children this young it is probably a good idea to limit them to one piece of paper. Letting them make several pictures sends a subtle message that there are no limits. As children colour, talk with them about friends at church, and tell them about Paul and Timothy.

Play shopping Over a few weeks save tins and food boxes at home. Leave the labels on tins and give them a rinse. Check them for any sharp edges. Stuff cereal and other food boxes with crumpled-up newspaper to make them stronger and seal them shut with sticky tape. Try to obtain one or two milk cartons or plastic milk containers. Collect egg boxes and cardboard fruit juice cartons as well.

Set out all the 'food' and provide paper carrier bags, shopping bags or a basket for children to pretend to buy food. When they have a full bag you can let them walk around the room, before bringing back their shopping and taking out the items so that someone else can have a turn. As the children take turns you can sing to them about friends, and you may be able to tell them some of the Bible story.

2s - 3s

Grocery shopping should prove very popular with twos and threes. You may be able to let one child be the 'grocer' who puts the things the shopper chooses into a bag or basket. They can pretend to take money at the end of the shopping.

Marble painting Find a shoe box, or other box of a similar size. Cut white paper to fit inside the base of the box. Write the child's name on the back of the paper, then place it in the box. Drop a few drops of fairly thin paint on the paper and place one or two marbles in the box. Let the child roll the box from side to side and back and forth. The marbles will roll through the paint and make a nice design. Most children need a bit of guidance so that they don't shake the box up and down – watch out for flying marbles! Also watch out for any children who have an unhealthy desire to put marbles in their mouths.

Children really enjoy marble painting. Two or three children may stand watching while another child paints. You can talk to them about fun times with friends at church, and tell them about Paul and Timothy.

Make a book about friends This activity was suggested for threes to fives in the first week of this unit. You can use it in the same way with a Polaroid camera or by gluing pictures and letting children decorate their own page.

Throw pegs into a basket Find a small plastic basket or washing-up bowl. Provide about ten pegs. Let children stand a few paces back and try to throw the pegs into the container. You will need to vary where children stand according to their ability. Take care not to make it a competition between children. Competition implies a level of skill – accurate throwing is not something most two and three-year-olds have practised.

Again, as this is a group activity, you will have opportunities to talk about friends in general, and Paul and Timothy specifically.

3s - 5s

Grocery shopping, marble painting and throwing pegs into a basket are all activities you can use with threes to fives today.

BIBLE STUFF · God made our world/God gives us friends

Week 3

Water play If you do not have a proper water play table for this activity, use a washing-up bowl, an old baby bath or any other suitable container. Make sure you cover the surrounding area with a plastic sheet. (It may be a wise move to invest in a durable waterproof ground-sheet from a camping equipment shop.) Newspapers on top of the plastic stop it pooling and becoming slippery.

You could put some boats in the water today, as well as a small collection of items that sink or float such as a pebble, a cork, a feather and a small ball. The children will be interested to see what different items do. As friends play together, tell them about Paul and Timothy.

Sort shapes This activity can be approached in two ways, depending on the maturity of your group. First the easier one: cut out shapes from six different colours of paper – red squares, blue triangles, green circles, etc. Make sure they are big enough for the children to handle easily: an eight centimetre square will be about right. Mix them up and let the children sort them into piles. They can sort by shape (if they know their shapes) or by colour if they prefer.

A slightly harder version of this activity is to cut a shape from each of the colours. You would then have six squares, each of a different colour, six different coloured triangles and so on. The children can sort by shape first, then by colour the next time. The difference may seem small to you as an adult, but to some children the second version is significantly more difficult. As children help each other with this activity, you can tell them about how Paul and Timothy helped each other teach people more about Jesus.

Group Time

2s - 3s

As was suggested two weeks ago, you may want to call the children to group time with a song. Perhaps today you could use the words, 'I am glad, I am glad, (child's name) is here today.' You could either sing this to each child after they are seated in the circle, or get them all to stand together away from the group area, and ask them to come and sit down when they hear you sing their name.

It shouldn't be too difficult to get the children to tell you about marble painting and playing shopping. Try to emphasize the friendship aspect of being involved in these activities. After you tell the story of Paul and Timothy, say a prayer thanking God for friends (children and grown-ups) and thanking God that we can work together to help people know more about Jesus.

As you wait for parents, bring out the basket and pegs, and let children take turns throwing two or three pegs into the basket.

3s - 5s

You may want to use one of the songs suggested for the younger group to call children to group time. 'I am glad' and 'I have a good friend' both involve singing a child's name. Most children really enjoy hearing their name used in this way.

Again, conversation shouldn't be difficult, and in the context of happy exchanges about friends doing things at church you can tell the story of Paul and Timothy.

As you wait for parents you can let the children throw the pegs into the basket or bring out the shape sorting game again.

GOD GIVES US FRIENDS — WEEK 3

Take Home!

PAUL AND TIMOTHY (ACTS 16:1-5; 2 TIMOTHY 4:9-18)

Aim
To help the children learn that friends work together; that they can tell people about Jesus together; that friends don't have to be the same age.

Bible verses
Paul and Timothy worked together. (Acts 16:3)
Paul loved his friend Timothy. (1 Corinthians 4:17)
Paul and Timothy taught people about God. (Acts 16:4)

The story
Paul loved Jesus. He went to lots of different towns to tell people about Jesus. He wanted to help many people love Jesus like he did. One day Paul visited a town and met a young man named Timothy. Timothy loved Jesus. A lot of people in the town knew Timothy and they liked him very much.

Paul was ready to go to some other towns. He asked Timothy to go with him to tell people about Jesus. Paul and Timothy became good friends. They worked together for many years to help people learn more about Jesus.

Sometimes Paul went to one town and Timothy went to a different town. When they weren't together, Paul wrote letters to Timothy. He told him how to teach the people. He told Timothy that he missed him. He liked it when Timothy was able to be with him.

Paul and Timothy were very good friends. They liked working together to tell people about Jesus.

Activity suggestions

Make shakers
You can make shakers for your baby with empty plastic drink bottles or empty film canisters. (You can usually get film canisters from anywhere that develops film. If you use them, make sure you seal the lid securely, as they will undoubtedly go into your baby's mouth!) Put a small amount of salt, rice, lentils, uncooked pasta or even one or two coins in the shakers. Make three or four, each with a different sound.

Throw pegs into a basket
Get about eight or ten pegs, and a small container such as an empty ice cream carton, a small basket or a cardboard box. Let your child stand back from the container and try to toss the pegs into it. How far back they stand depends on how old they are and how well they can throw.

This is not a game for the sake of competition. Very few under fives can throw with great accuracy! It is a fun activity that encourages their development. As you play, talk about things that friends do together. Tell your child about Paul and Timothy.

Write a letter
Paul wrote to Timothy. Help your child draw a picture or write a letter to a friend or family member who does not live locally. Let your child help you to post it.

God Gives Us Friends Week 4

JESUS VISITS FRIENDS (LUKE 10:38-42; JOHN 11; 12:1-8)

Aim To help the children know that Jesus had friends and that he spent time with his friends.

Preparation

In this session we concentrate on the well-known episode from Luke 10. For more background concerning the friendship Jesus shared with Mary, Martha and Lazarus, read John 11 and 12:1-8.

These passages tell us about part of the very human life of Jesus. He, like us, had friends. The Gospels lead us to believe that Jesus had visited the home of Mary, Martha and Lazarus on several occasions. Perhaps they had travelled to see him and hear his teaching whenever he was anywhere near Bethany. Although they were undoubtedly devoted followers of Jesus (Mary and Martha both address him as 'Lord' in John 11), they were also on level ground with him. They were his friends.

The link between Mary sitting at Jesus' feet and our own need to have a contemplative side to our lives is beyond the capabilities of under fives. But the fact that Jesus had friends is well within their grasp. Not only did he have friends, but he spent time with them. He visited their homes and talked with them. This is what we want to communicate today.

This story will help us teach the children more about Jesus. It is good for them to know that he had friends. In a small way it will help them to further understand that Jesus is Immanuel, God with us. As they get older and begin to learn how important it is that Jesus was truly human, perhaps they will understand it more readily because they have always known about the human side of Jesus' life.

For us as adults, this story helps us further appreciate that Jesus has been where we are. When we enjoy strong friendships and times of relaxation and laughter, we know that Jesus enjoyed them as well. Jesus also had friends who turned their backs on him and didn't want to be associated with him in difficult times. He knows how that feels as well. It is good to know that in both the good and the bad times of our lives and friendships, Jesus knows and understands.

He walked where I walk,
He stood where I stand,
He felt what I feel,
He understands.
God with us, so close to us, Immanuel.
Graham Kendrick

'*Father, thank you that you have given us friendships for enjoyment and relaxation. Help us to make the most of them. Thank you, too, that sometimes friendships can be very significant in our lives and in the using of our gifts for you. I pray that my friendships with the children and their parents will not only be for pleasure, but that they will matter in your kingdom. Amen.*'

Story Time

Bible verses
Jesus loved his friends Mary, Martha and Lazarus. (John 11:5)
Jesus went to Mary and Martha's house for dinner. (Luke 10:38)
A friend loves at all times. (Proverbs 17:17)

Week 4

Birth - 2s

Jesus went to different towns and villages to teach people about God and make sick people well. In a village called Bethany, he had some friends named Mary, Martha and Lazarus. Whenever Jesus went to Bethany he went to see them.

One day Jesus went to Mary and Martha's house for a meal. Martha was busy doing the cooking. Mary was sitting near Jesus, listening to what he was saying.

Martha said, 'Jesus, I am doing all the work. Can't you tell Mary to help me?'

Jesus said, 'Do not worry Martha. Mary has chosen to do something important. She will remember the things I tell her.'

Jesus loved his friends Mary, Martha and Lazarus. He liked going to their house.

3s - 5s

Jesus went to different towns and villages to teach people about God and make sick people well. In a village called Bethany, he had some friends named Mary, Martha and Lazarus. Whenever Jesus went to Bethany he went to see them. Sometimes he went to their house for dinner.

One day when Jesus was at Mary and Martha's house, Martha was busy cooking and cleaning. Mary was sitting near Jesus, listening to what he was saying.

Martha said, 'Jesus, I am doing all the work. Mary is only sitting there. Can't you tell Mary to help me?'

Jesus said, 'Martha, Martha. You are worried about the cooking and the cleaning. It's all right for Mary to sit with me today. What she is doing is important. She will remember the things I tell her.'

Jesus loved his friends Mary, Martha and Lazarus. He liked going to visit them.

Teaching Activities

As we teach the story today, let's emphasize the positive and joyful nature of Jesus' friendship with this family at Bethany. It was a natural part of his life, yet it became significant to his ministry. For when Jesus raised Lazarus from the dead (a part of the story which isn't really within the reach of under fives) many people believed in him and followed him (John 11:45). Our friendships with one another and with the children are a natural part of our lives. That is a good thing. But we never know what greater importance God places on such relationships.

Babies

Make a box toy with pictures of food Use an empty tissue box (a tall square one as opposed to a rectangular one) to make a picture toy. Stuff the box with crumpled up newspaper to make it stronger. Cover the sides, top and bottom with coloured paper and glue a picture of food on each of the six sides. Try to find simple, easily recognizable pictures – a piece of fruit, some vegetables, a glass of milk or a plate of meat and potatoes. If you want to make the toy more durable, cover it with sticky-backed plastic so the babies can't tear the pictures off.

As you thank God for food to eat, you can tell a baby about Jesus having a meal with his friends.

Make a texture book or board Obtain several flat items with different textures, such as cotton wool, velvet, satin and sandpaper. You can mount them all on a board (a very strong piece of cardboard will do), or glue each one to a piece of card and put them together to make a book.

BIBLE STUFF   *God made our world/God gives us friends*   **45**

Week 4

As you guide a baby to feel the different textures, say thank you to God for fingers to feel.

Play with wooden and plastic spoons Bring some large wooden and plastic spoons for babies to play with. Make sure they are the big ones with long handles, as opposed to small plastic eating spoons – some older babies may get confused and think they are going to be fed! Older babies will enjoy tapping the spoons together, and even younger babies will be able to hold the handle of a spoon.

As babies play with the spoons you can tell them about Martha preparing a meal for her friend Jesus, or sing the songs about friends that you have been using in this unit.

Play with a rocking horse or other rocking toy If your church has a parent and toddler group you may have access to a rocking horse or some other kind of rocking toy. Older babies will enjoy this for a change. It will obviously need one teacher to supervise, so you can only do this if you have enough staff. As babies rock, sing to them about friends, or about rocking.

Toddlers

Use the texture book or board with toddlers today, as well as the tissue-box picture toy. Bring wooden spoons for the children to play with, and some plastic bowls or small saucepans so they can pretend to mix and cook. You may also want to consider the following ideas.

Marble paint This activity was suggested for the twos and threes last week. You can use it in exactly the same way. If you think that marbles will be jolted out of the box too easily, you can use a golf ball instead. The effect of the picture is not quite as good, but the fun is in the doing, not the end result.

'Clean' the room Bring several dusting cloths and a 'squirt bottle' with water in it. Help the children squirt water onto various surfaces in the room and 'clean' them with the dusters. This can include doors, cupboards, tables – anything that won't be damaged by having water squirted on it. You may want to say to the children, 'It is all right for you to squirt this bottle because I gave it to you. You should never squirt a bottle without asking a grownup first.'

If you have a child-sized broom or dustpan and brush, let the children use these as well. This will probably be a new experience for toddlers, so they may need a good bit of guidance at the beginning. As the children clean you can talk about cooking and cleaning for visitors, and about Jesus going to Mary and Martha's house.

2s - 3s

Even twos and threes will enjoy looking at a tissue-box picture cube and feeling different textures. For this age group you may want to mount the textures on strong card so they can see them all at once, and touch more than one at a time. Cleaning the room is an activity the children usually enjoy – the dusting cloths are usually fairly wet by the end. Bring wooden and plastic spoons, plastic bowls for mixing, and one or two aprons for the children to do pretend cooking in the home corner. You may also want to include the following activity.

Make a food picture Provide a paper plate for each child, and several pictures of various kinds of food. Let each child choose some pictures to glue on their plate. On the edge of the plate write 'Jesus had dinner with his friends'. As the children look at the food pictures and choose which ones they want to glue, you can thank God for good food and tell part of the Bible story.

3s - 5s

The threes to fives will enjoy cleaning the room and making food pictures today. Bring spoons, bowls and aprons for them to use in the home corner. If you have access to plastic plates, bowls and cutlery, bring these and a table cloth so the children can lay the table for guests. If not, just use the usual tea set you have in the home corner.

Week 4

Consider including the following two additional activities.

Make a 'feel bag' of textures Use the same textures suggested for other age groups, but have two samples of each. Put one set into a cloth bag where the children can't see them. Alternatively, you can tape the lid on a shoe box, and cut a hole in one end for children to stick their hand in and feel the objects. Spread out the other set of textures. Let each child choose a texture, then put his or her hand in the bag or box to try and find the matching texture by feeling.

As children do this activity, thank God for hands to feel, talk about other things we can feel, and discuss the difference between rough and smooth.

Mix coloured water Bring several clear plastic cups or bottles, a jug of water and red, blue and yellow food colouring. Put a small amount of water in a cup, then add a few drops of food colouring. The children will enjoy watching the water change colour. Then mix two different colours of water and see what you get. Have a spare container ready for tipping the coloured water into so you can start again. Some children will be so fascinated by this that they will want to see you do it several times.

Be careful not to call it magic – even though the children cannot understand the scientific principles of light and colour, they do not need to be misled by thinking it is magic. As you mix colours and make new ones, thank God for all the beautiful colours he has made.

Group Time

2s - 3s
When the children have finished tidying up, you can sing an action song to start group time. Get the children to follow you around the room as you sing, 'It's fun to march around the room, around the room, around the room. It's fun to march around the room, around the room with our friends.' (Tune of 'Mulberry Bush'). You can sing it several times, substituting words such as walk, dance and hop for 'march'.

When you have got the children sitting down you may need to do a few action rhymes to settle them. Then you can begin the normal group time activities of talking, telling the Bible story, praying and singing.

As you wait for parents to arrive you can give out the food pictures. As you do so, point out one or two kinds of food for all the children to look at.

3s - 5s
Start group time as suggested for twos and threes. After you have told the Bible story and included singing, conversation and prayer, you could bring out the coloured water again, or the texture bag. You could also hand out the pictures, looking at and talking about food as you do so.

GOD GIVES US FRIENDS — WEEK 4

Take Home!

JESUS VISITS FRIENDS (LUKE 10:38-42; JOHN 11; 12:1-8)

Aim
To help the children know that Jesus had friends and that he spent time with his friends.

Bible verses
Jesus loved his friends Mary, Martha and Lazarus. (John 11:5)
Jesus went to Mary and Martha's house for dinner. (Luke 10:38)
A friend loves at all times. (Proverbs 17:17)

The story
Jesus went to different towns and villages to teach people about God and make sick people well. In a village called Bethany, he had some friends named Mary, Martha and Lazarus. Whenever Jesus went to Bethany he went to see them. Sometimes he went to their house for dinner.

One day when Jesus was at Mary and Martha's house, Martha was busy cooking and cleaning. Mary was sitting near Jesus, listening to what he was saying.

Martha said, 'Jesus, I am doing all the work. Mary is only sitting there. Can't you tell Mary to help me?'

Jesus said, 'Martha, Martha. You are worried about the cooking and the cleaning. It's all right for Mary to sit with me today. What she is doing is important. She will remember the things I tell her.'

Jesus loved his friends Mary, Martha and Lazarus. He liked going to visit them.

Activity suggestions

Play with wooden or plastic spoons
Give your baby some large wooden or plastic spoons from your kitchen utensil drawer. As they play with them, tell the story of Jesus visiting Mary and Martha. For older babies, toddlers and older under fives, you may want to add saucepans and plastic mixing bowls. You may need to say to your child, 'You may play with these today because I have given them to you, but you may not get them out of the kitchen cupboards yourself'. Otherwise, your child might think all the kitchen utensils are fair game!

Make instant whip
Let your child help you prepare instant whip as a treat for a special snack or for dessert at tea time. Let them pour in the milk and use the whisk or rotary beater. Choose a time when you are not in a hurry, as it will take longer than when you make it by yourself.

Tell your child about Jesus going to eat at Mary and Martha's house.

BIBLE STUFF